The Pacification of
Central America

DATE DUE

The Pacification of Central America

Political Change in the Isthmus, 1987–1993

JAMES DUNKERLEY

VERSO

London · New York

First published by Verso 1994
© James Dunkerley 1994
All rights reserved

Verso
UK: 6 Meard Street, London W1V 3HR
USA: 29 West 35th Street, New York, NY 10001-2291

Verso is the imprint of New Left Books

ISBN 0 86091 423 2
ISBN 0 86091 648 0 (pbk)

British Library Cataloguing in Publication Data
A catalogue record for this book is available from the British Library

Library of Congress Cataloging-in-Publication Data
Dunkerley, James.
The pacification of Central America / James Dunkerley.
p.   cm.
Includes bibliographical references (p.   ).
ISBN 0-86091-423-2 — ISBN 0-86091-648-0 (pbk.)
1. Central America—Politics and government—1979– 2. Central
America—Social conditions—1979– 3. Central America—Economic
conditions—1979– I. Title.
F1439.5.D86   1994
972.805'3—dc20

Typeset by Solidus (Bristol) Limited
Printed and bound in Great Britain by
Biddles Ltd, Guildford and King's Lynn

To Penny, Dylan and Alice

Contents

CONTENTS

List of Abbreviations

AMNLAE	Asociación de Mujeres Nicaragüenses Luisa Amanda Espinosa, Nicaragua
APP	Area de Propiedad Popular, Nicaragua
ARENA	Alianza Republicana Nacionalista, El Salvador
ATC	Asociación de Trabajadores del Campo, Nicaragua
CACIF	Comité Coordinador de Asociaciones Agrícolas, Comerciales, Industriales y Financieras, Guatemala
CACM	Central American Common Market
CCN	Cruzada Cívica Nacional, Panama
CD	Convergencia Democrática, El Salvador
CEC	Comunidad Económica Centroamericana
CIA	Central Intelligence Agency, USA
CIAV	Comisión Internacional de Apoyo y Verificación, UN/OAS
CNR	Comisión Nacional de Reconciliación, Guatemala
CODESA	Corporación Costarricense de Desarrollo S.A., Costa Rica
CONADI	Corporación Nacional de Inversiones, Honduras
CONAVIGUA	Coordinadora Nacional de Viudas Guatemaltecas, Guatemala
COPAZ	Comisión para la Consolidación de la Paz, El Salvador

CORNAP	Corporación Nacional de Privatización, Nicaragua
CPR	Comunidades de Poblaciones en Resistencia, Guatemala
DCG	Democracia Cristiana Guatemalteca, Guatemala
DEA	Drugs Enforcement Agency, USA
EC	European Community
EPS	Ejército Popular Sandinista, Nicaragua
ERP	Ejército Revolucionario del Pueblo, El Salvador
FDP	Fuerzas de Defensa de Panamá, Panama
FDR	Frente Democrático Revolucionario, El Salvador
FMLN	Frente Farabundo Martí para la Liberación Nacional, El Salvador
FNT	Frente Nacional de Trabajadores, Nicaragua
FPL	Fuerzas Populares de Liberación, El Salvador
FSLN	Frente Sandinista de Liberación Nacional, Nicaragua
FUSEP	Fuerzas de Seguridad Pública, Honduras
GAM	Grupo de Apoyo Mutuo, Guatemala
GAP	Gobierno de Amplia Participación, El Salvador
INC	Instancia Nacional de Consenso, Guatemala
IPM	Instituto de Previsión Militar, Honduras
MAS	Movimiento de Acción Solidaria, Guatemala
NSC	National Security Council, USA
OAS	Organisation of American States
ONUCA	United Nations Observer Mission in Central America
ONUSAL	United Nations Observer Mission in El Salvador
PAC	Patrullas de Autodefensa Civil, Guatemala
PARLACEN	Parlamento Centroamericano
PDC	Partido Demócrata Cristiano, El Salvador
PN	Partido Nacional, Honduras

LIST OF ABBREVIATIONS

PNC	Policia Nacional Civil, El Salvador
PNR	Plan de Reconstrucción Nacional, El Salvador
PR	Partido Revolucionario, Guatemala
PRTC	Partido Revolucionario de Trabajadores Centroamericanos
PVP	Partido de Vanguardia Popular, Costa Rica
UCN	Unión Centrista Nacional, Guatemala
UNHCR	United Nations High Commission for Refugees
UNO	Unión Nacional Opositora, Nicaragua
UPEB	Unión de Paises Exportadores del Banano
URNG	Unión Revolucionaria Nacional Guatemalteca, Guatemala

Preface

The aim of this survey is to provide a summary depiction of the main political developments in Central America over what may yet transpire to be the most complex and dynamic period of its modern history. The fact that the survey is organized in three parts – the present essay; a select chronology; and some other appendices – makes clear that it is not a work of closely considered and integrated scholarship. However, because much of the information reproduced here has only been available either in specialist publications or – more frequently – in piecemeal fashion, even a very synthetic and artisanal assessment would seem to be justified. Those who consult the notes will see that I have relied very heavily on the weekly *Central American Report*, which is published in Guatemala City by Inforpress Centroamericana. I am particularly grateful to the Inforpress team, which has maintained an exemplary publication through very taxing times. Tony Bell, Victor Bulmer-Thomas and Rachel Sieder have been extremely generous with advice, loans of material and comment, but none is responsible for the probable errors and definite oddities that follow.

OCTOBER 1993

Every man's hand almost was against his brother, at least his heart, little regarding anything that should cement and might have a tendency in it to cause us to grow into one. All the dispensations of God, his terrible ones – he having met us in the way of his judgement in a ten years' civil war, a very sharp one – his merciful dispensations, they did not, they did not work upon us but we had our humours and interests; and indeed I fear our humours were more than our interests. And certainly as it fell out, in such cases our passions were more than our judgements.

OLIVER CROMWELL TO THE FIRST PROTECTORATE
PARLIAMENT, 4 SEPTEMBER 1654

The Pacification of
Central America

The 1980s were miserably harsh years for Central America. Precise and reliable figures will never be available for measuring the human cost of the region's three civil wars. A fair but conservative estimate would be 160,000 people killed and two million displaced during the decade; it is the scale, not the precision, that impresses.[1] The longest of these conflicts – that in Guatemala – began over thirty years ago and remains unresolved as of October 1993. However, the Guatemalan crisis of May/June 1993 gave at least some grounds for expecting serious efforts towards peace – if only in the sense of a cessation of hostilities – despite the numerous false dawns that have afflicted that country since the counter-revolution of June 1954.

Should such efforts take hold they would build on the resolution of the civil wars in Nicaragua (1981–90) and El Salvador (1980–91), where laborious and intricate negotiations terminated conflicts of great brutality and bitterness. As the succession of meetings, confusion of proposals and muddle of events came to dominate the coverage of these countries' affairs in the metropolitan media, interest in them naturally began to decrease. The tendency was, of course, abetted by the simultaneous collapse of Communism and the outbreak of other civil wars, the terrifying images of which should serve to remind us of the merits of what Cromwell called 'settling and healing', even if this is achieved in unheroic manner, at the cost of dreams, and through the concession of often vital interests.

I am here using the rather ungainly word 'pacification' because – at least in English – it carries a feeling of temporality, an attachment to mood and some sense of approximation – maybe even interchange-ability – between subject and object.[2] At the same time, it is not a word as fraught with casual overuse and normative subversions as is 'democracy'. One should, though, be mindful of the fact that this is a word that appeared in English, Spanish and French between 1460 and 1483 – at a time of civil war and conquest, for which it was quite frequently employed as a euphemism as well as signifying the ending of war, assuaging of discontented parties and negotiating of settlements.[3]

Cortés employed it in both senses, and las Casas contrasts the native Americans' 'pacific possession' of their lands to 'conquest' in his invective against the excesses of Cortés and his like.

In 1573 Phillip II banned the use of the word 'conquest' from official accounts of 'discovery' in the Americas and elsewhere.[4] Three years later the provinces of the Low Countries signed 'The Pacification of Ghent' as a treaty in union against the Spanish crown. Whilst the Esquipulas II regional peace treaty of August 1987 lacks Ghent's warlike articles against the outsider, it is certainly similar in its concern for internal accord and settlement. Moreover, the Esquipulas treaty opened a six-year period during which fighting was gradually brought to a halt on terms that fell short of outright victory for any of the (local and external) protagonists, and although the settlements that followed derived from much negotiation and diplomacy, they were also influenced by sharp military exchanges right up to the end.

Such an observation applies best to the cases of Nicaragua and El Salvador. In Guatemala peace will not be the result of any military stalemate between the guerrillas of the Unión Revolucionaria Nacional Guatemalteca (URNG) and the army of the state, which has succeeded in a strategic subjugation of the radical challenge whilst failing to eliminate the rebels or eradicate the popular sympathy often felt – but rarely displayed – towards them. In the cases of Honduras and Costa Rica there has been nothing approaching civil war, but since these are all small countries with close relations events elsewhere have pressed – both directly and as relayed through US policy – sharply on their domestic affairs. Hence, although we will concentrate here on the main sites of conflict, some attention must be paid to Honduras – where, after all, the great bulk of the Nicaraguan Contras was stationed – and Costa Rica, which, despite possessing a civic culture so adjusted to the rule of law that notions of 'pacification' might seem abusive, has experienced important internal stress in addition to playing a key role in regional diplomacy.

The issue of whether this still incomplete process of negotiation, demilitarization and institutional reform is tantamount to 'democratization', let alone 'redemocratization', is not a central concern here. The range of democratic theory from slogan to sophistry has become so great that any serious effort to apply it to a region such as Central America would require a lengthy peregrination through the definitions. However, definition does provide more than consolation for those unhappy with the intricacies of history or the menace of fickle opinion. So, for the purposes of drawing a provisional margin we might note the observation – made in the context of a review of Central America – by John Peeler that contemporary everyday usage ... interprets ... democracy as a regime with near universal adult suffrage, periodic competitive elections in which opposition parties have a reasonable chance to win, and widely respected freedoms of speech and political organization ... such a polity [is] a liberal political system legitimized by the appearance of a democracy.[5]

A somewhat looser, but more explicitly critical, understanding is given by Richard Fagen, who sees democracy as involving 'effective participation by individuals and groups, a system of accountability, and political equality'.[6] This, plainly, might well be very different from the pattern of liberal democracy currently being instituted in Central America and elsewhere, but it is scarcely a recipe for the formalist collectivism so comprehensively disgraced by its practice in the Soviet bloc.

Many conservative commentators are inclined to dismiss critiques of liberal democracy – or democracy as liberalism – as more or less stealthy reformulations of a redundant class-based politics. Yet in recent years it has been less a class than a cultural critique of the universal pretensions of liberalism that has attracted most attention.[7] In terms of historical analysis this approach has been compellingly developed for Italy by Robert Putnam, whose emphasis upon varied traditional forms of cultural participation revives some of the 'political culture' arguments raised by Almond and Verba and quite widely considered redundant by the 1980s.[8] In terms of advocacy it could find few more succinct proponents than Yoweri Museveni, unelected president of Uganda, who resists the metropolitan campaign for liberal democracy in Africa on the simple grounds that 'multi-party democracy works in Europe where social divisions are horizontal, based on class. In Africa the divisions are vertical, based on tribe. Multi-party democracy in Africa leads to tribalism and division.'[9]

Such a comment does not properly apply to Central America – with the exception, perhaps, of parts of highland Guatemala – but it serves as a useful qualification to the tendency to triumphalism which now so often attends the propagation of liberal democracy and which has been particularly shrill in the case of Central America, where this was long projected by Washington as a conflict with Communism. Indeed, this tendency is now so strong that it extends well beyond right-wing circles and has, I sense, contributed to the diminished interest in Central American affairs as these are seen to 'conform to type'.

Caution, clearly, is required, even in the wake of extraordinarily brutal autocracies. The much-quoted observation by Adam Przeworski that 'the process of establishing a democracy is a process of institutionalizing uncertainty' is both true and necessary.[10] However, for poor people scratching a living in poor countries wracked by violent conflict existence is already so shot through with uncertainty that such a proposition is neither so risky nor so attractive as the observation implies. In such cases the utterance of judicious pieties as if there were always a tomorrow faces stiff competition from even the most mediocre populist rhetoric of deliverance.

Another declaration by a northern academic recently quoted approvingly in a volume on Central American politics runs as follows:

> Lying is the most nefarious political offence ... Untruths destroy the possibility of creating common perceptions of political events, and therefore can fracture a political community at all levels of participation ... Political falsehoods create many social events out of one empirical occurrence, threaten community cohesion by opening up the possibility of value conflicts ... tend to produce erratic politics, and this ... impoverishes individuals and societies.[11]

One need be neither a postmodernist nor a Jesuit to see that all sorts of difficulties lurk beneath the surface of this quite plausible – if rather insolent – requirement of honesty in public affairs. Montaigne, who, of course, lived a good part of his life in the midst of war, cautions us thus:

> ... as soon as you have established the frontiers of truth and error with that fine brain of yours and then discover that you must of necessity believe some things even stronger than the ones which you reject, you are already forced to abandon these frontiers.

He ends the same essay with an even tougher stricture:

> Vainglory and curiosity are twin scourges of our souls. The former makes us stick our noses into everything; the latter forbids us to leave anything unresolved or undecided.[12]

It is not that there can be any serious disputation about the need for candour and transparency in public life everywhere, but rather that this requirement is still tightly latched to quite markedly puritan notions of personal conduct. These are in themselves highly contestable, but they become positively oppressive in circumstances under which for the simple purposes of daily survival ordinary folk have learned how to stay silent, dissemble, manifest ignorance and tell untruths. What, after a decade of clandestinity, death squads, raids and interrogations, is a secret? When do secrets become lies, even in the cultural sense celebrated by Rigoberta Menchú?[13]

In a recent suggestive essay that confronts the kind of complacency that concerns me here, Laurence Whitehead has excluded Central America (together – for distinct reasons – with Mexico and the Caribbean) from a South American pattern of 'democracy by default'. The major features of that broad tendency – which may be seen as an unfinished 'third cycle' following those of 1944–48 and 1955–62 – are the absence of impulses to autocracy and external intervention (previously the Cold War and the Cuban Revolution); growing disenchantment on the part of local entrepreneurs and foreign capital with the statism and inefficiency of military regimes; the severe deflation of military confidence by the debt crisis; and the 'deradicalization' of progressive forces caused by exceptionally severe repression for which they were utterly unprepared.[14] Few of these factors may usefully be applied to Central America, where, as Rodolfo Cerdas has observed, authoritarian regimes were in no sense the product of any populist excess or reformist ambition that might have exhausted civil tolerance or loosened the bonds of tradition.[15]

This is an important – but often ignored – point. Just as Central America did not become submerged in dictatorship during the 1970s as the result of any 'populist' phase of political economy identified (at that time) by Guillermo O'Donnell as a harbinger to bureaucratic authoritarianism, so also it is now patently not acquiring liberal democratic institutions as a consequence of developments in what Marcelo Cavarozzi calls the 'state-centred matrix' ('import-substitution industrialization'; the closing of the economy; state regulation of markets; 'moderate' inflation rates).[16] The economies of these countries are too small to register anything more than the faintest echo (or flimsiest emulation) of the structures and policies established in Brazil, Argentina or Mexico. One must look much more directly at politics to find the core factors in the isthmian pattern of regime transition, which is in a number of ways quite distinct from that in South America.

An inescapable complicating factor in assessing this short and highly charged period is the strength and breadth of swings in analytical mood – as distinct from the events to which they are a response. This, of course, has been particularly marked on a global scale since mid 1989, not just at both ends of the political spectrum but also in that notional 'centre' which sought to benefit from the excessive ambition of a right made dizzy by the sight of a future without an antagonist as well as from the debilitated left's disarray. Within Latin America the echoes of this erraticism are further confused by regional sub-patterns, which, with nearly two dozen different polities, are not just intricate but also prone to give – by virtue of serial repetition – an exaggerated impression of movement. These shifts can be on a relatively long cycle. In May 1989

7

Whitehead noted the existence of just two dictatorships (Chile and Paraguay) whereas fifteen years earlier there had been just three constitutional governments (Colombia, Venezuela, Costa Rica), but he ended his piece by identifying 'the shallowness of fashionable sloganizing about a supposed "worldwide march towards democracy"'.[17] In May 1993 the Santiago correspondent of the *Guardian*, Malcolm Coad, writing two days after President Serrano had grasped dictatorial power in Guatemala, noted that this followed the impeachment of two elected presidents (Collor, Brazil, in December 1992; Pérez, Venezuela, in May 1993), the overthrow of another (Aristide, Haiti, in October 1991) and the mutation of a fourth into an autocrat (Fujimori, Peru, in April 1992). The despondency caused by these developments stood in stark contrast to the euphoria prevailing only a few months earlier in the wake of the removal of Pinochet and Stroessner from (presidential) power, the ending of the Salvadorean civil war, and the initial mirage provided by neo-liberalism in the time-lag between the fall in inflation rates and that in a range of other economic indicators.[18] It is perhaps unsurprising that comment on and speculation about Cuba manifest these mood-swings to a high – and, it must be said, probably disproportionate – degree.

There has been little conservative academic analysis of the post-Esquipulas period in Central America. This is to be expected; a large proportion of a quite modest right-wing academic output in the mid 1980s was preoccupied with direct anti-Communist tasks that are now redundant. Where there is some vestigial urge to espy radicalism – such as in Jesse Helms's remarkably successful campaign to freeze US aid to Nicaragua in 1992–93 – this has been supported by empirical evidence and analytical assumptions of the most dubious kind. The region has also largely ceased to be an echo-chamber for wider debates – even that over Cuba – and the local disputes between what we might call oligarchic corporatism (traditional conservatism) and liberal radicalism (modern mercantilism) are not yet sharp enough nor sufficiently driven by ideology to attract much attention abroad. For the traditional right the image of a region embracing the formalities of liberal democracy provides a reassuring reprise of the oligarchic and North American dominion of the first three decades of the century, when neither Bolshevism nor Mexican statism seriously impaired the view. For neo-liberals there is slight interest in historically poor, low-inflation and open economies that offer scant opportunity for manifesting the empowering and enfranchising qualities of the market. As we shall see, privatization campaigns have been launched in most countries, but these have tended to take the form of specific interests rather than a general ideology, predictable instances of rigged tendering, asset-stripping and punitive expropriation provoking often powerful – if only sometimes successful – popular response. Whitehead's criticism of the neo-liberal prospectus for Latin America as a whole – and even elements of his 'social democratic' qualification – remain valid for the isthmus.[19]

The general defensiveness of comment on the left abroad clearly reflects the downturn in interest (and solidarity) in metropolitan societies.[20] More than three years after the Nicaraguan elections one is not taken aback to come across references to 'the Sandinista bourgeois elite' although there are still few who have the confidence to assert that

> [the] Sandinista decision to endanger the revolutionary process by holding national elections in the midst of war and economic disintegration was not made on the basis of an examination of the conditions of the working class, the peasantry, and the urban and rural poor ... [a] fundamental strategic mistake.[21]

James Petras and Morris Morley – the authors of this statement – are at pains to criticize (unnamed) 'dogmatic Marxists', but their own perspective is so persistently dismissive of non-economic matters that the general tendency of the North American left to over-react to ('bourgeois') behaviouralism is taken to an extreme. Matters of political economy assuredly remain crucial and enforce clear structural limits to the human condition in Central America, but the region has also thrown up remarkable instances of agency and initiative on both sides – the FMLN's offensive on San Salvador in November 1989; the Sandinistas' decision to hold elections; the Guatemalan crisis of mid 1993 – for which structuralist explanations are of distinctly partial value.

There has certainly been a sanctionable over-obfuscation of language by erstwhile radical intellectuals in a perceptible shift away from what might be called the 'cosmovision' of Marxism. However, this tendency is not simply the result of cowardice and prostitution, and it will not be dissolved by name-calling.[22] In my view, an especially important local factor for the disenchantment of the left (largely abroad) has been the end of fighting, which had served for so long as a veil for maximalism. By this I mean that it was (and remains) difficult to divorce from the image of people prepared to kill and die the idea that they can only do so for the highest ideals. The conflation of fighting and idealism that is often essential for combatants also infects committed onlookers even when, as in the case of Petras and Morley, they possess strong political disagreements with the people they would prefer to win. The disappointment when combat ceases and haggling pragmatism sets in is correspondingly fierce, and perhaps goes some way to explaining structuralist stubbornness in explanation.

Noam Chomsky, the most distinguished North American radical writing on Central America – amongst other matters – stands in little danger of being accused of Leninist truculence despite his constant attacks on Washington's policies. Indeed, in one key respect, he is at complete variance with Petras and Morley for his recent books contain minimal mention of resistance abroad to US power.[23] Opponents are neither blamed nor praised because they are strictly secondary in Chomsky's analytical approach and political concerns. Although a libertarian by conviction, he is a bona fide structuralist. As Jean Piaget, one of the founding fathers of that school, has commented of Chomsky's theory of linguistics, he does not begin his analysis with piecemeal evidence or procedures but universals (or 'wholeness'). Piaget is right that this approach 'completely inverts logical positivism' and that 'it does not bother [Chomsky] in the least' that this is the case.[24] It can be seriously argued that such an epistemology is equally – if not more – strongly evident in Chomsky's political writing, where the fundamental predicate (or assumption) is less conspiracy theory than the (structured) omnipotence that needs must lie behind this. There is no need to present or discuss countervailing evidence; this may be screened out as analytically irrelevant and politically confusing. Structural 'logic' even accounts for absences and silences: 'Washington failed to disrupt the 1984 election in Nicaragua by terror'.[25]

It may be objected that Chomsky is a most unworthy target of criticism because of his solitary and heroic efforts to wage a campaign against US imperialism. However, this has been a campaign with footnotes, and one that addresses intellectual concerns as well as popular engagement. Intellectually, its reliance on inductive methods leaves it very vulnerable to charges of empirical clumsiness – a charge that is particularly dangerous in view of the extraordinary aggregation of material deployed by Chomsky to persuade his audience.[26] Politically, the insistence upon imperialist prowess and wrong-doing is intrinsically pessimistic and liable to demobilize the very audience that it is clearly intended to win over. The effect of successive illustration of imperial injustice may initially be cathartic in the sense that it provides a dissident strand of a logical positivist society with the relief of having evidence for its convictions. But there is also the risk – from the viewpoint of the left – that this becomes merely a litany, an excuse as well as an explanation, disturbing in its contemporary approximation to predestinarianism. For our present purposes, Chomsky's scrupulous aversion to prescribing policies alternative to those that prevail is less important than the fact that his method effaces precisely those features – the contradictions and failures of US policy and the politico-military resources of the Central American left – that should be at the heart of an explanation of the region's politics between 1987 and 1993 that puts history before polemic.

This last point requires brief qualification because one does not need to subscribe either to Chomsky's marginalization of the Central American left or to Petras's assertions of its insufficiencies to see that the picture is mixed. We will look again at the experience of the Sandinistas and the Salvadorean FMLN since these forces – the first withdrawing from office after a decade, the second entering the legal sphere after a dozen years – remain central to the political landscape of their countries. However, the record in Guatemala, Honduras and Costa Rica is quite distinct.

In Guatemala the URNG, founded in February 1982, has failed to build the capacity for a strategic military offensive over ten years, whilst no openly radical organization can exist above ground for any length of time before its members are liable to be executed. The result has been a parallel process of frequent but inconsequential schism within clandestine groups and the construction of 'non-ideological', civic groups – usually around human rights issues – in public. The 'left' as such, then, seems both weak and defensive, but if it has indeed remained embattled in military terms, and perforce absent from legal politics, these facts may well have exaggerated both the image of defeat and the degree to which popular forces will need to regroup before they can make a political impact. The remarkably strong spontaneous popular mobilizations of 1978, 1985, 1990 and 1993 – the first two in conditions of severe repression; the latter two at significant risk to participants – suggest greater potential than appearances might justify.[27]

The experience of Costa Rican radicalism could barely be more different since the left has been permitted to contest open elections – up to 1975 under the guise of non-Communist fronts; thereafter unhampered by anti-Communist laws – and to organize with constitutional guarantees. Despite the fact that the Partido de Vanguardia Popular (PVP; Communist Party) played a key role in establishing Costa Rica's welfare system in the 1940s, neither it nor other, smaller radical organizations have made any significant impact on the electorate, never winning more than 8 per cent of the vote for Congress or 3.5 per cent for that for the presidency in thirty years.[28] As a result, the PVP, set up in 1931, underwent important splits in 1983 and 1986 as first the Nicaraguan Revolution and then conservative economic policies taxed its programmatic resources. The party appeared to have regained both confidence and energy at its 1990 congress, but it was bouncing back from its worst-ever election result (9,178 votes – 0.6 per cent of the turn-out – in February 1990) and subsequently failed to establish a profile in the campaign against the sharp neo-liberalism of the new Calderón administration.[29]

The Honduran left has not even had a putative 'golden age' after which to hanker, has never been permitted to contest a national election, and, despite giving rise to four guerrilla groups in the early 1980s,[30] lacked the logistical capacity for anything beyond kidnapping and low-scale sabotage. By the turn of the decade its leadership was publicly disavowing armed struggle and returning from exile without any negotiated settlement or real expectation of breaking out of the political periphery. Indeed, the Honduran left may be most guilty of the 'rhetorical excess' which Cerdas perceives as a critical weakness of regional radicalism.[31] However, in turning to the more substantive features of this period we will find that the discursive inheritance of the left is but a subordinate feature.

The Economy

The travails of the Central American economies may be traced through Appendices 2 to 6. During the period of most intensive conflict in the isthmus, 1981–92, the GDP per capita of Latin America as a whole contracted by 7.3 per cent whilst that of the countries of the Central American Common Market (CACM) fell by a full 15 per cent. It is true that boycotted and besieged Nicaragua's economic disaster is responsi-ble for a good portion of this average – it contracted by over 38 per cent – but even if we set Nicaragua aside, the GDP per capita of the other economies of the region fell by nearly 11 per cent.[32] GDP per capita growth is non-existent in Nicaragua; very slight and erratic from 1984 in El Salvador; very slight from 1987 in Guatemala; very slight and erratic throughout the decade in Honduras; and only modest in Costa Rica from 1987.

The performance of individual economies and the considerable difficulties of regional trade were undoubtedly related to the pattern of military conflict, notably in Nicaragua, where this was so great that it is effectively impossible to distinguish and measure, but also in El Salvador, where on the eve of the final truce the government assessed direct damage to be $329 million, indirect damage at $708 million, and reconstruction costs at $1,826 million.[33] However, one must also identify earlier indebtedness, a crisis in the price of regional staples, and the general world recession as important factors. In 1980 debt service was 16 per cent of regional exports; by 1985 it had risen to 46 per cent; and at the end of the decade it was still 30 per cent despite significant negotiation over rescheduling.[34] Indebtedness, it should be stressed, directly affects governments' budgets, debt service accounting for 27 per cent of that in Guatemala in 1992, 27 per cent of Costa Rica's and 33 per cent of Honduras's for 1993.[35] The period of greatest concern to us (1987–93) is also marked by a collapse in the price of coffee, by 60 per cent between July 1989, when the International Coffee Organization halted its quota system, and May 1993, when the world price for washed arabicas was at its lowest for seventy years.[36] Given that between 1982 and 1987 Central America cultivated an average of 765,000 hectares of coffee and exported 8.6 million bags a year, it is scarcely surprising that the fall in this market has had a severe effect.[37] Overall regional losses since the collapse of the quota system have been put at $1 billion.[38] This, too, has had a sharp impact on government finances as tax revenues from coffee contracted, in the case of El Salvador from $955 million (35 per cent of internal state revenue) in 1986 to $253 million (8 per cent) in 1990.[39]

The world market in bananas – the region's other traditional export crop – has not been as seriously affected, but the imposition in December 1992 by the European Community (EC) of a two-million-ton quota with a 20–25 per cent tariff on Latin American fruit to take effect from July 1993 represents a major threat. According to the Union of Banana Exporting Countries (UPEB) this will cost 174,000 jobs with estimated losses of 900,000 tons per annum, or roughly $1 billion.[40] The UPEB claim is not, of course, disinterested and may be taken as exaggerated, but the EC's policy must certainly disrupt the region's economies in the coming period.

Basic grain production was hit in the early 1990s by the fierce drought caused by irregularities in the El Niño current, the effect being to increase the trend towards imports of US wheat (nearly 600,000 tons in 1990), away from traditional consumption of maize (still 70 per cent of cereal production), and to an ever sharper food dependency ratio. Between 1970 and 1986 cereal imports had risen from 15 per cent to 21 per cent of total consumption (32 per cent in Costa Rica and 27 per cent in El Salvador), not least because after the Nicaraguan Revolution US food aid to the other countries of the region increased by a factor of fifteen (to $120 million in 1990).[41] Between 1989 and 1992 regional production of cereals fell by 15 per cent, imports rising by 32 per cent.[42] Since most of the latter entered under US PL480 soft food loans the issue of political conditionality combines with that of food security, which has declined everywhere with the partial exception of Honduras.

These shifts have been accompanied by a significant increase in *maquiladora* industry (local assembly of largely imported inputs for re-export, usually with generous tax breaks). Nicaragua is the only country not to have been seriously affected by this expansion which saw *maquila* exports rise from $285.2 million in 1987 to $1,570 million in 1992.[43] Indeed, *The Economist* explained the failure in June 1993 of Guatemalan entrepreneurs to support Jorge Serrano's coup largely in terms of the impact a US economic boycott would have on the non-traditional market-garden exports and *maquiladora* production, especially at a time when prices of traditional exports – sugar and cotton as well as coffee – were so low.[44]

Another shared regional experience – including by Nicaragua under FSLN government – has been the application of orthodox stabilization policies in an effort to reduce inflation. Here the region has followed a general Latin American pattern – one that analysts increasingly identify as critical to the experience of regime transition even when they are sharply opposed to the social costs of these policies. If we exclude Nicaragua, which entered a hyperinflationary spiral in 1985, the average regional figures for inflation are – in Latin American terms – relatively modest and stable (1987 – 12.05 per cent; 1988 – 15.6 per cent; 1989 – 16.3 per cent; 1990 – 35.65 per cent; 1991 – 16.67 per cent; 1992 – 12.97 per cent). Control of monetary policy has not been absolutely strict, but on those occasions where it has lapsed – in Guatemala, Honduras and Costa Rica in 1990 – it has generally been rectified. The case of Nicaragua cannot be taken as directly comparable, but even there we should note that the strict measures imposed by the Sandinistas in 1988 reduced the level of inflation from 33,548 per cent to 1,689 per cent, and when this started to spin out of control again the following (election) year at 13,500 per cent, Violeta Chamorro's team cut it back very rapidly.

After 1987, then, Central America was governed by regimes with quite similar goals in this area – a fact that encouraged renewed interest in economic integration as progress was made towards political peace-making under the Esquipulas accords. Here, of course, political will is very much a necessary rather than a sufficient condition, and a legion of obstacles – some mentioned already – face the successful creation of the new Central American Economic Community (CEC) formally established at the presidential summits held in Antigua in 1990 and San Salvador in 1991.[45] Starting with a liberalization in the trade of agricultural products – notably weak for a region so strongly based on

agriculture – this process has advanced very much on the basis of free
trade agreements, especially once incorporation into the North American Free Trade Agreement (NAFTA) was shown to be unrealistic in the
short term.

Central America has similarly echoed tendencies elsewhere in its
adoption of privatization policies. In Nicaragua these have been at the
core of national life since the February 1990 elections, and we will
return below to their negotiation in that charged period of *concertación*.
Public sector enterprises under civilian control in Guatemala are many
fewer – one result of the historically lower levels of taxation – leaving
little scope for sales, the most important of which has been a third of
the state airline Aviateca in 1989.[46] Costa Rica is at the other end of the
scale, but the complicated legal status and strong political influence of
the state's quasi-autonomous corporations and their subordinate enterprises have presented many barriers, even to the Calderón administration for which privatization was a key policy. In this case it took the
insistence of the World Bank and the Interamerican Development Bank
that sale be a condition for release of final structural adjustment loans
before the National Assembly approved the privatization of Cementos
de Pacífico and Fertilizantes de Centroamérica in March 1993. Both
companies were operating at a profit but carried large debts and had
previously belonged to the sprawling CODESA public corporation that
is closely identified by the private sector with the interventionist excesses
of the 1970s.[47]

The political impact of privatization in Honduras has been sharper,
partly because of the enthusiasm of the National Party (PN)
government of Rafael Callejas elected in November 1989, partly
because the sixty companies controlled by the state holding company
(CONADI) were more vulnerable to US conditionality and military
ambition, and partly because it came to affect not just the ownership
of individual rural properties but also the general legal basis for the
tenure of land. Legislation to permit sales of specific state enterprises
was first passed in February 1989, but the Liberal Party administration
of Azcona de Hoyo resisted the much-touted privatization of the
national cement company, making this an election issue and enhancing
the profile given to it by Callejas once he took office. There is, then,
some irony in the fact that when the cement company was finally sold
off, in September 1991, it was to the (eminently public) Instituto de
Previsión Militar, infuriating COHEP, the national business association.[48] Moreover, the Honduran case demonstrates that privatization
is by no means a cost-free process of flogging off nationally owned
assets at prices readily determined by market forces. Within six months

of Callejas's inauguration, the cost of legal fees and discounted prices in selling CONADI enterprises was over L45 million ($10 million) – a matter that also raised popular protest.[49] Government proposals to privatize the massively indebted public health system in mid 1991 were soon overtaken as an issue by the general agricultural law, passed in March 1992, which effectively halted state intervention, strictly limited the grounds for expropriation, and made generous concessions to foreign investors. The law signalled the end of thirty years of a highly variable but sometimes critical state commitment to agrarian reform.[50] The subsequent auctioning of cooperatives in the Bajo Aguán area aggravated conflict between *campesino* organizations but only encouraged Callejas both to introduce a general law facilitating privatization and to prepare for the sale of profitable public sugar, power and telephone firms.[51] It is extremely doubtful if Callejas was able through this policy to reduce the prebendary qualities of the Honduran state by much, and he seems to have been inadvisably zealous in imposing privatization on the land question despite the deep division of the popular movement in the countryside. As so often in Honduran politics, it was less a case of a concerted conflict than of aggregate effects and tendencies diminishing room for manoeuvre.

Outside of Nicaragua, El Salvador is the country where privatization and the pursuit of free market policies have had the highest profile in recent years. With leftist forces effectively excluded from legal politics during the 1980s, open policy debates very much revolved around disputes between the Christian Democrats (PDC), who fiercely defended the nationalized agencies and companies hastily assembled in league with the US in the first years of the civil war, and the radical right headed by ARENA, which, supported by powerful entrepreneurial interests, not only championed free markets but also inveighed against the corrupt practices that had come to infect the public sector. This latter campaign struck a chord with the public, and, in fact, after ARENA came to office in June 1989, Alfredo Cristiani began his programme not with the banks and coffee wholesaling agency so important to the merchant elite, but on the land.[52] Here the revival and great advertisement of the 'land to the tiller' programme of titling small plots provided a relatively uncontroversial and popular (50,000 titles without any expropriations in thirty months) introduction to the much more vigorously contested sale of the country's six banks nationalized in 1980 and, to even sharper popular discontent, the privatization of public outpatient services in the capital's main hospital.[53]

Despite demonstrations, Cristiani announced at the end of 1991 a second stage of this programme targeting sugar, cement and electricity companies as well as the San Bartolo free trade zone, which accounted for nearly a third of traditional exports.[54] However, disputes within ARENA, the political costs of some 10,000 job losses, and the removal of services such as food regulation (at a time of cholera) as well as the poor records of the companies slated for sale greatly reduced the programme's impetus after mid 1992, even to the extent that the National Privatization Commission was closed a mere five months after its establishment.[55] The only profitable public enterprise sold in that year was the Hotel Presidente; others were either contracted out or simply closed down. It may well be that the establishment of the San Salvador stock exchange in April 1992 – in the midst of the implementation of the first phase of the peace agreement – marked the apogee of the mercantilist campaign opened in 1989. Henceforth the response of unions and opposition parties no longer so daunted by repression will at least require a much more detailed and expansive justification for such actions. It is also possible that the country's principal capitalist groups have obtained sufficient assets and fulfilled enough of their initial ideological ambitions in this area for public policy subsequently to be less emphatic and conflictive.

Even the qualified privatizations realized by Central American governments in the early 1990s have extended the gap between a restricted private affluence and a generalized public squalor that was already formidably wide. Here, once more, Central America conforms to the sub-continental pattern insofar as the establishment of liberal democratic systems has occurred at a time of deepening poverty for the mass of (potential) citizens, and in some key respects that transition has accelerated pauperization. In fact, even the strictly average GDP per capita growth rate for the region between 1987 and 1992 is lower, at 0.4 per cent, than was that for the period 1980–87 (0.41 per cent).[56]

With the signal exception of Costa Rica, the Central American countries embarked upon the process of pacification with indices of infant mortality, life expectancy at birth, access to potable water, malnutrition, percentage of GDP invested in housing, illiteracy and persons per doctor that were worse than those for Latin America as a whole.[57] Nearly eighteen months after the election of Violeta Chamorro the state of Nicaragua's poor was still the worst in the isthmus with some 50 per cent of the labour force un- or underemployed and over 69 per cent unable to meet basic food needs.[58] Elsewhere the modest official figures for open urban unemployment between 1987 and 1992 (Costa Rica: 5.3 per cent; El Salvador: 9 per cent; Guatemala: 7.9 per cent; Honduras: 8.4 per cent) obscure the much deeper reach of 'marginalization' and impoverishment. This is true even of Costa Rica, where in 1990–91 some 27,821 families were classified poor for the first time, an 18.4 per cent increase. In Honduras, the other country not directly immersed in conflict, the College of Economists assessed the number of the country's inhabitants living in poverty to have risen from 67 per cent to 73 per cent between 1989 and 1992.[59]

It is not just the economic crisis but also the civil wars that have uprooted families or traditional bread-winners from their homes, deprived them of familiar employment and thrown them into the euphemistically termed 'informal economy'. This, moreover, has been more than a national and regional process, many thousands fleeing as economic or political refugees to the USA during the 1980s. The greatest concentration has been from the three countries at war – El Salvador, Guatemala, Nicaragua. In the case of El Salvador there were, according to conservative estimates, 690,000 immigrants in the USA in 1989. That year their remittances of dollars home exceeded $759 million – 15 per cent of GDP and three times the revenue from coffee exports. Figures from the same source for Guatemala have 50,000 immigrants remitting $248 million in 1989; and for Nicaragua 255,000 remitting $59.8 million.[60]

This is a comparatively new phenomenon – in 1980 remittances from some 170,000 Salvadorean immigrants in the US amounted to just $74 million (or 6.2 per cent of total exports). Over the subsequent decade family remittances to these three countries covered two-thirds of the fall in export revenue and foreign investment – a most impressive demonstration of the degree to which labour has become a regional export.[61]

Women

Such a development has not gone unnoticed on the streets of Los Angeles or Washington.[62] However, less attention has been paid to its impact on domestic and family structures and activity in Central America itself. The sources for this are still slight and very uneven, but it would seem clear that it has encouraged greater involvement of women in public labour even though the growth of female participation in the regional labour force has constantly outstripped that of males since World War II: 3.47 per cent against 2.68 per cent in 1950–70; 4.28 per cent against 2.72 per cent in 1970–80; and 4.4 per cent against 3.06 per cent in 1980–90.[63] Women now officially comprise 31 per cent of the regional labour force, and the figure would be appreciably higher if the 'informal' sector were included. (Recent attempts to measure this put women at 57 per cent of 'informal' workers in Nicaragua, 53 per cent in El Salvador, and 38 per cent in Costa Rica).[64] It is probable that migration of all types has increased the extent to which women have become heads of household; in the case of El Salvador this is estimated to be 33 per cent; in Managua 30 per cent; in Guatemala City 21 per cent.

There is perhaps no area where these phenomena conjoin in more critical fashion than in the field of health and childcare – rarely high on the agenda of political analysts but increasingly recognized as a factor at the core of 'public opinion' when that public lacks both state provision and private means. (Here the example of Cuba may well have been over-sloganized, but it behoves marketeers to explain why Caribbean Communism should have taken the route of 'health in one country', even before ethical, fiscal and operational crisis struck the US public health system so resoundingly.) According to UNICEF, by the end of the 1980s 100,000 of the one million Central Americans born in 1983 were dead, largely because of cuts in health spending, and an equal number were wounded or incapacitated as a more direct result of the civil wars. If all the countries had achieved an infant mortality rate equal to Costa Rica's – 24 per 1,000 live births, instead of the regional rate of 93 – 190 lives would have been saved daily. This contrast is sharpened further still by the fact that in Guatemala 11 women died in every 10,000 live births, and only a quarter of sexually active Guatemalan women use contraception.[65] By 1990 Guatemalan public health was on the verge of collapse. Despite nominal increases in both budget and share of overall government spending, the real allocation for 1990 barely exceeded that of 1986. The capital's Roosevelt Hospital – once famed throughout Latin America – had effectively run out of supplies, could not replace staff, and was being systematically pillaged by politically appointed administrators. This pattern was evident in the rest of the country's thirty-five hospitals, which owed over $5 million to suppliers whilst the Health Ministry was $22 million in debt and Congress was refusing to release sufficient funds.[66]

Another facet of such pressures – and their political importance – may be found in the scandal of child-trafficking in Honduras. The discovery in April 1993 of the frozen body of a minor in a freight wagon at Cortés – the cadaver apparently being intended for organ transplants – brought to a head an eighteen-month campaign by Deputy Rosario Godoy de Osejo over child-trafficking rings, principally for illegal adoption abroad, in which she implicated the Callejas presidency.[67] According to official figures, 800 Honduran children went missing in the 1990s, many in 'fattening houses' (run by lawyers) prior to adoption. These houses would seem to be made necessary by the fact that 57 per cent of all Honduran children are malnourished and 70 per cent suffer respiratory diseases. It is also telling that a trade (in human beings) so closely associated elsewhere in Latin America with the children of victims of military repression should be on the upsurge in Honduras under a constitutional administration. In this case a country that had experienced relatively few adult disappearances for political causes in the 1980s was subjected to a shock of shame and outrage which greatly exceeded that traditionally provoked by its habitually high levels of official swindling and preferment.[68]

In the light of developments of this type Central American women have unsurprisingly taken a higher political profile in recent years. It is certainly the case that this profile is still publicly centred on their role as widows or relatives of victims of repression. And one might usefully extend this description to Violeta Chamorro, but it takes on a greater sense of resilience in the examples not only of Rigoberta Menchú but also of Nineth de García, leader of the Guatemalan Grupo de Apoyo Mutuo (GAM), and Rosalina Tuyuc of CONAVIGUA, the national widows' association. Whilst perhaps no more than 15 per cent of the URNG's fighters are women, the figure was at least 30 per cent for the FMLN, amongst whose principal leaders have been Nélida Anaya Montes (FPL; died 1983), Nidia Díaz (PRTC), and Ana Guadalupe Martínez (ERP).[69] Moreover, as the FMLN transforms itself into an orthodox political party, one might expect a continued autonomous voice from organizations of relatives of the victims of repressions such as FECMAFAM as well as from returned refugees, 53 per cent of whom were women.

Nonetheless, one is mindful of the experience of Nicaragua, where after more than a decade of radical administration, advances made by women were quite modest, not least insofar as only three held ministerial posts under the FSLN.[70] As Daniel Ortega noted in his report to the first Sandinista congress in July 1991, despite the introduction of a divorce law and legislation regulating the responsibilities of fathers, 'one has to recognize that ... we were not able, for a number of reasons, including ideological ones, to articulate as a party a concrete programme consistent with our ideas'.[71] In this respect, it is worth observing that the forerunner of the national womens' organization AMNLAE was an explicitly anti-dictatorial body (AMPRONAC) not dissimilar to the more recent bodies established elsewhere, and that AMNLAE itself had no proper leadership elections until March 1991. From 1987 the FSLN leadership promoted the slogan 'women are not a sector', which militated directly against a feminist agenda, dodged the issue of equal pay, and became increasingly mealy-mouthed about abortion – always a controversial matter, even for a president whose wife – Rosario Murillo – has nine children (and at least one maid).[72] This, however, must be set against the decidedly reactionary ethical positions of the Chamorro government, which was far more conservative on social policy than on its political alliances.

Cholera

The cholera epidemic that struck Peru in January 1991 and had reached Guatemala by July of that year was exceptional by any standards, Central America not having suffered a major outbreak since 1856. Frequent use of the phrase 'time of cholera' in articles and books cashes in on the popularity of Gabriel García Marquez's novel *Love in the Time of Cholera* (1985), set in the last great South American outbreak of 1895 and, in Gerry Martin's words, an 'unmistakable portrait ... of the end of an era'.[73] However, the borrowed titles have not been completely spurious for cholera has historically carried cataclysmic connotations and often attended moments of political change as well as social decomposition, not least in Britain in 1832 and 1848 but also in Guatemala in the late 1830s.[74] The image of an exceptionally potent disease capable of killing an adult within a few hours has no doubt fortified a sense of helplessness and fatalism. However, as early as 1849 *The Economist* called it a 'disease of society' and doctors in Melbourne mistakenly feared that only an outbreak of cholera would prompt the construction of sewers. The connection between the disease and the quality of water was decisively established with the publication of John Snow's *On the Communication of Cholera* in 1855, and it has rarely been difficult to trace the speed of subsequent epidemics to poor sanitation, lack of potable water, and insufficient personal hygiene, even if the immediate cause is often in greens or shallow-water fish, both commonly sold in Central American streets.[75] These factors are largely dependent on infrastructure that is either very poor or entirely absent in most of this region, as evidenced by the figures for the share of the population with direct access to water: Guatemala – 38 per cent; El Salvador – 52 per cent; Honduras – 50 per cent; Nicaragua – 45 per cent; Costa Rica – 96 per cent. As a result of this, the expectations in early 1991 were that the particularly fierce El Tor strain of cholera that had affected 170,000 Peruvians and killed more than 1,200 in the space of nine weeks would put some 600,000 Central Americans at risk.[76]

By mid January 1992 the region had registered somewhat fewer than 10,000 cases with under 200 deaths, the greatest proportion occurring in Guatemala.[77] However, in the first fortnight of May there was a sharp resurgence. The number of cases doubled in Honduras (to thirty) and quadrupled in Nicaragua (to over 100) whilst those in El Salvador rose by 1,000 (ten deaths) and in Guatemala by an equal amount (a total of seventy deaths).[78] Costa Rica registered its first five cases. The question as to why this sharp increase took place is of interest and might also alert us to the scope of explanation beyond inadequacies in infrastructure. This itself was immediately criticized, not just in terms of lack of potable water and sewerage but also for the failure of mayors and local authorities to spend sufficiently – or in some cases at all – on chlorination. On the other hand, it is probable that nearly a year after the initial outbreak the populace had ceased to observe precautions tedious even for those with domestic water supply. With relatively few cases, cholera had apparently lost its terror. Possibly more important still, the second outbreak took place after Holy Week, a time of holidays, travelling, indulgence and, of course, large crowds at Easter processions. Finally, one might suggest that the long lull aggravated the confusion caused by an infection that, after incubation of twelve to forty-eight hours, shocks with its rapid development of acute diarrhoea, dehydration and loss of voice. As with child diarrhoea – so closely linked to malnutrition – this may be rapidly treated without specialist help using oral rehydration salts, a formula of salt, sugar and potassium developed in the mid 1970s. However, whilst supply of salts was in most countries adequate, this was not the case in terms of the level of popular health education, which was just as important, for instance in persuading mothers to continue breast-feeding children with diarrhoea or rural communities that they should not cover up suspect cases out of either shame or a desire to protect the market for their garden produce.

As with AIDS, which first appeared in 1985 and killed nearly a thousand Central Americans over the following seven years, cholera was preventable at a low price, and whilst it affected many more people, it was eminently curable.[79] The record of the epidemic of the early 1990s is as mixed as the political conditions under which it occurred. On the one hand, there is inadequate infrastructure, very low health and education budgets, and a significant level of elite disdain and popular superstition. Against this, there has been important regional coordination and appreciable energy invested by health professionals and activists in campaigns of the type pioneered in Cuba. Perhaps most notable of all, as in most of Latin America, there has been very little political agitation around the management of the epidemic.

The Military

All three civil wars of the 1980s lasted for at least eight years, and each involved frequent operations across at least one international frontier. The armed forces or police of all the regional states became embroiled to a greater or lesser degree, as did those of the US, Cuba, Mexico and Argentina. For a while, in the mid 1980s, the threat of a truly regional war was strong. Appendix 9 tabulates this escalation. The number of troops in Central America rose from approximately 48,000 at the end of the 1970s to nearly 200,000 in 1985. At the same time, notwithstanding a quite effective arms embargo imposed on both Guatemala and Nicaragua by the US, there was a notable increase in weaponry, equipment and aircraft in the region. Although we lack reliable information for contemporary possession of weaponry, it is clear that the process of regional demilitarization has been slow and most uneven. In 1991 official regional troop strengths still stood at 179,000 despite some slimming down of the Costa Rican paramilitary forces and the radical reduction of the Ejército Popular Sandinista (EPS) by over 30,000. The main reason for this lack of movement was the expansion of the Salvadorean, Guatemalan and Honduran armed forces at a time when the armed threats against them were either diminishing or non-existent.

In the case of El Salvador this is explained in part by the imminence of a negotiated demilitarization in which elite battalions would be 'traded' for FMLN units in a process of linked demobilization, which eventually took place throughout 1992. However, in all these countries one observes a fierce reluctance on the part of the high command to cede the considerable powers accumulated over the previous decade not simply in terms of public prestige, hardware and economic holdings but also over civil society at large, as applied through the traditional mechanism of conscription. As late as mid 1990 the Guatemalan and Honduran armed forces were forcibly conscripting hundreds of youths in sweeps undertaken with little apparent care for the response of either public opinion or the law.[80] The fact that President Callejas had formally declared the last Nicaraguan Contras to have left Honduran soil on 18 April 1990 made the subsequent pressganging seem to be nothing more than a deliberate assertion of the military's *fuero*, or de jure as well as de facto independence.

The extent to which the USA had encouraged the militarization through aid is fully evident in Appendix 8. However, after the demobilization of the Contras even the Bush administration, which had insisted on keeping the Nicaraguan rebel force intact throughout 1989, became annoyed with the Honduran military. This may have been because the high command in Tegucigalpa had generally become too accustomed to Pentagon support during Reagan's anti-Sandinista crusade, enabling them both to play the anti-Communist card and to seek comparability with the aid given to their rivals in the Salvadorean military who faced a genuine guerrilla threat. However, senior Honduran officers appear to have been constructing a business empire well beyond the customary corporate perquisites of housing, hospitals and insurance. In June 1989 popular protests obliged President Azcona de Hoyo to rescind after a week his decree granting over 1,000 officers lifelong rights to a car, chauffeur, bodyguard and health care abroad, not least because the military had already cornered a third of the national budget.[81] Later in the year the over-valuation of the dollar on the important San Pedro Sula black market threatened to cause a major financial upset until the intervention of Colonel Reinaldo Andino Flores, commander of the 105th Infantry Brigade, who not only effectively set the national exchange rate for the Central Bank but also countermanded the central government's prohibition of informal trading in dollars. Neither the executive nor Congress made any official statement.[82] Congress also did not dare impede the chief of the armed forces, General Luis Alfonso Discua Elvir, from having the republic's laws altered so that he could serve a second term from the start of 1993.

One possible reason for this was that Discua now presided over such an extensive economic network that few politicians felt able to cross him. We have already noted the ability of the military's business corporation, IPM, to buy the profitable national cement company in the face of the protests of a capitalist class alleging incorrect expenditure of taxpayers' money. In addition to this, IPM had already acquired a bank, an insurance company, a radio station (classical music) and a funeral parlour.[83] IPM's 1992 profits were estimated at $40 million, and talk of an 'armed bourgeoisie' extended well beyond the circles of liberal intellectuals. The Voice of America stated: 'Honduras is an army with a country, not a country with an army', and US Ambassador Crescencio Arcos engaged in sharp public exchanges with Discua over the need to reduce the size and cost of the military.[84] Early in 1993 Washington eventually lost patience and cut aid to the almost nominal sum of $2.7 million.

As Appendix 8 indicates, pressures of this type were not applicable in Guatemala or Nicaragua, which had anyway substantially reduced its army. In the case of Guatemala a military institution also possessed of important economic interests and capable of sustaining a major counter-insurgency campaign without much US support will undoubtedly resist any settlement along the lines agreed for El Salvador at the end of 1991, and, as we will see, it is likely to be internal rather than external pressure that will loosen what are as much ideological and operational convictions as economic interests.

A more general problem, with or without a formal process of demobilization, is the surfeit of weaponry circulating in Central American society, the extensive motivation and capacity to commit crime, and the tenuous hold of professional police forces in the region. This is true even of Costa Rica, where well-supported charges of torture were levelled against the OIJ specialist police unit in 1989, and where by mid 1991 it was possible to identify eleven different public police and paramilitary bodies, incorporating a staff of some 20,000, as well as fifteen private security firms.[85] Yet this apparent erosion of the civic and neutralist ethic of the post-1948 Costa Rican state failed to halt a series of armed actions and kidnappings, such as that of eighteen members of the Supreme Court for three days in April 1993 by five masked men who pretended to be Colombian drug-traffickers but were, in fact, hoping to raise funds so that one of their number, an ex-police officer, might get a liver transplant.[86]

In Nicaragua it has been estimated that early in 1992, after two years of demobilization covering some 60,000 troops (including 33,000 Contra and 'Recontra' fighters of the 'Resistance') there were still 100,000 people either possessing or with direct access to automatic weapons. Crime was rising six times faster than the birth rate, and more than a hundred people had been killed in armed clashes over the previous six months.[87] By mid 1993 a state of near-rebellion reigned in the northern and central zones of the country, requiring major and highly controversial operations by the army to contain armed bands composed of veterans of both sides in the civil war of the 1980s. In such a context it is hardly surprising that elements of the EPS might illegally sell SAM missiles to comrades in the Salvadorean FMLN or, indeed, that the FMLN itself might maintain in Managua substantial caches of these missiles and other weapons after the deadline had passed for the surrender and destruction of these within El Salvador under the peace agreement.[88] In fact, inside El Salvador itself the agreed dismantling of the repressive Guardia Nacional and Policía de Hacienda paramilitary forces in March 1992 had the predictable effect of triggering an upsurge in crime, for which the very partially trained and lightly armed civilian police in the process of being set up was poorly prepared.[89] Nor should one forget those exceptional cases of police officers who honourably performed their duty in the face of insuperable odds and sometimes at the cost of their lives at the hands of 'colleagues'. Amongst these one ought to mention at least José Miguel Mérida Escobar, chief of the Guatemalan police's homicide division, who was killed by a death squad in August 1991 having implicated an army agent attached to the president's office in the murder of the anthropologist Myrna Mack, stabbed to death in September 1990.[90] Another officer, Vilma Arévalo, narrowly escaped such a fate in the wake of inquiries into the March 1990 murder of Nahamán Carmona, one of many Guatemalan street children done to death in a wave of vigilante violence so naturally spawned by years of political repression.[91]

United States Policy

Central American politics cannot be properly understood as a simple reflection of US power. Yet neither is it possible to comprehend regional affairs without close reference to Washington's policies, however secretly these may be formulated and however clumsy their implementation. Moreover, it is worth reminding ourselves that 'Washington' amounts to a great deal more than the White House or even the often theatrical exchanges between executive and legislature.[92] The Iran-Contra scandal, which broke in November 1986 and had the effect of accelerating peace plans within the region, underlines the important role of executive agencies such as the CIA and the National Security Council (NSC), especially when legislative constraints encouraged the presidency not just to indulge in 'covert operations' – barely remarkable in Central America during the 1980s – but to make an important strand of foreign policy dependent precisely upon those operations (sale of missiles to Iran with transfer of the resulting revenue to Nicaraguan Contra forces, support for whom was invigilated and legally restricted by the US Congress). In addition, one should note the enhanced influence of the Department of Defense in a region where diplomacy was often a veil rather than an authentic instrument of policy, where three civil wars were being fought and US military aid of $1.8 billion had been disbursed over a dozen years.

During the period that concerns us here Central American politicians of all colours were confronted with a particularly testing balance of forces in Washington. Whilst it is certainly the case that the Iran-Contra affair damaged the second Reagan administration's Central American policy by diminishing its prestige with the US public, international opinion and a Democrat-controlled Congress, it should not be forgotten that this occurred in the broader context given by the establishment of the reformist Gorbachev regime in the USSR. The motions towards detente made by Moscow increased Washington's confidence precisely at a time when it had been badly wrong-footed over Nicaragua. As a result, the Reagan government was distinctly reluctant to amend – let alone withdraw from – a set of notably aggressive policies developed for the region. Moreover, as William Leogrande has noted, 'Reagan's minimum and maximum objectives in Nicaragua were the same. The continued existence of the Sandinista government was simply unacceptable; nothing short of its removal would do.'[93]

The consequence was a form of stand-off, which prevailed between the signing of the Esquipulas accord in August 1987 and the inauguration of George Bush in January 1989. During this period Washington was unable to halt regional negotiations but it proved readily capable of limiting their scope and, indeed, the expectations vested in them. However, when Bush came to office, 'he was prepared to accept co-existence if the Sandinistas would live up to their commitments under the Esquipulas accord'.[94] As we shall see, this more qualified approach – the fact that there was some modest space between Bush's minimum and maximum aims – revived the possibilities of diplomatic and political initiative that had previously been nullified by Reagan's consistent subjection of these unavoidable formalities to an ultimatumist veto.

The first tangible expression of the shift was in the signing of the 'Bipartisan Accord on Central America' with the Democratic leaders of Congress in March 1989, just a few weeks after Bush's inauguration. This deal was brokered by the new secretary of state, James Baker, who had a reputation for 'taming the ideologues' under Reagan, and the new assistant secretary of state, Bernard Aronson, who was largely ignorant of Latin American affairs but as an erstwhile speechwriter for Walter Mondale as well as an active supporter of Contra aid represented a safe but moderate replacement for the pugnacious Cold Warrior Elliott Abrams. In essence, this agreement recognized both the implausibility of maintaining Reagan's Nicaraguan policy and the fact that this had dangerously curbed US flexibility elsewhere in the isthmus. The 'bottom line' deal was that the Contras would be kept in place and provided with 'humanitarian' aid in Honduras until after the Nicaraguan elections in February 1990. During this period of just under a year the White House would liaise closely with Congress, giving a clear signal that it accepted the possibility of a settlement with Managua, where, perhaps predictably, Daniel Ortega called the agreement a 'terrorist package'.[95]

Both the strength of Reagan's policy and the depth of divisions over the Contras even before the revelations in November 1986 of Colonel

North's secret activities meant that some form of domestic rapprochment over Nicaragua was required once Reagan was gone. This was not, though, necessary for El Salvador, where bipartisan consensus had been much stronger, in part because the US was trying to maintain rather than overthrow a government, in part because it had organized the holding of a string of elections as well as pumping in huge quantities of military aid (but relatively few advisers and no infantry), and in part because one of those polls had yielded in José Napoleón Duarte a president who was a faithful US ally and an open (if impotent) opponent of the ultra-right. All these factors made for the plausible presentation of – and occasionally even the belief in – a country governed by altruistic centrists equally distanced from and besieged by reactionary extremists in the landed oligarchy and army and their radical counterparts in the FMLN, aided and abetted through the familiar ideo-logistical supply-line from Morazán to Managua to Havana to Moscow. One of the earliest and fiercest (but never seriously substantiated) charges made against the Sandinistas by the Reagan team was that they were exporting revolution by backing the Salvadorean FMLN. Throughout the 1980s such accusations varied in emphasis and were gradually replaced by direct attacks on Managua's internal regime, but they still appeared in the 1989 Bipartisan agreement, and they did help to furnish Democrats with a convenient basis for hawkishness as they reaped domestic political advantage by assailing the administration over the Contras.

The widespread violation of human rights in El Salvador had troubled Congress in the early 1980s, and for a while it required Reagan to certify that the position was improving before each tranche of military aid was approved. But the president had soon unilaterally ceased doing this, and as the war settled into a familiar low-intensity pattern without widely publicized massacres of the type witnessed in 1979–83, there were few efforts to stage an authentic debate, still less to challenge the administration's realpolitik or the Pentagon's operational needs between 1984 (when Duarte was elected) and 1989. The event that terminated this concordat was the FMLN's completely unexpected offensive of November 1989 which rocked the regime in El Salvador and provoked a brutal backlash from the armed forces that shocked international opinion but failed to defeat the rebels. We will return to this briefly below, but it is worth noting here the impact of the fighting within the US, where Senators John Kerry and Edward Kennedy proposed a bill in January 1990 to cut off military aid entirely despite the fact that similar moves in both Houses had failed at the height of the offensive when images of slaughter were much starker.

(Although so also was the possibility of precipitating military defeat by withholding funds – a preoccupation rehearsed in January 1981.)[96]

The Kerry–Kennedy 'end the war' bill was replaced by another, drafted by Connecticut Senator Christopher Dodd, who had long criticized Reagan's policy but had been persuaded by the Bush team to give the new Salvadorean government of Alfredo Cristiani the opportunity to exercise its electoral mandate won in the spring of 1989.[97] Dodd now drew up a bill designed to make US aid conditional upon an improvement in the government's human rights record and tangible progress in negotiations with the FMLN. In August 1990 what had become known as the Dodd/Leahy bill survived attempted amendments by the administration in committee and froze one-half of US military aid of $85 million to El Salvador, making the entire amount subject to withdrawal should San Salvador refuse to engage in peace talks with the rebels, but also providing for its complete restoration should the FMLN do likewise, direct operations against civilians or receive logistical support from other countries.[98] On 19 October 1990 the US Senate voted 75–24 in favour of the reduced package, and although the Bush administration chafed, it had to accept the congressional initiative. A policy that had been based on bipartisan agreements even under Reagan had effectively come under the authority of the legislature. This, however, was by no means just the result of a more flexible team in the White House since there was now broad agreement across Washington (including the Pentagon) over the desirability of a settlement in El Salvador. Such a state of play resulted not simply from the military balance of forces within that country but also from the electoral defeat of the Sandinistas in February, which had provided a clear regional confirmation of the shifts in the global order. Perhaps most important from the North American perspective was the fact that these re-adjustments occurred in the wake of the US invasion of Panama on 20 December 1989, the consequences of which for Central American affairs remain extremely vital notwithstanding the disconcertingly peculiar political circumstances that surrounded it.

The Panamanian Crisis

William Leogrande's assessment of the invasion of Panama as being as successful for Bush as had been that of Grenada for Reagan is perfectly justifiable from both domestic and foreign policy perspectives; at least in the short term.[99] It does, however, mask a number of features of the two-and-a-half-year Panamanian crisis that presented Washington with considerable difficulties and occasionally acute embarrassment. This was true even after Christmas 1989, when US troops, having lost less than two score men and secured most of the country, had General Noriega bottled up in the Vatican's embassy, protected only by the nuncio and three nuns as he sought asylum. There, in front of a rapidly expanded press corps, the US forces blasted out high-volume rock music for seventy-two hours without interruption – an initiative described by a military spokesman as 'a way of introducing ambient sound to ensure the security of military communications'.[100] Whilst both the action and the excuse were characteristic of General Maxwell Thurman, the US commander, they reflect a wider failure of US nerve and sophistication. Such a reaction was also evident in the doling out of 44,000 Combat Infantryman Badges (when only 2,500 troops actually engaged in combat) and the award to soldiers evacuated with sprained ankles of medals that in World War II had been given only to troops experiencing at least thirty days and nights of combat.[101] Perhaps, though, it was the spectacle of the most powerful government on the globe indulging in an almost medieval demonization of the Panamanian tyrant that was as telling as it was unedifying.

Noriega, it may be remembered, was said by Pentagon sources to practise voodoo with vats of animal blood and entrails, to wear red underwear in order to ward off the evil eye, and to keep a witch's diary and a portrait of Hitler, in addition to manifesting the normal catalogue of deviant sexual practices and sadistic impulses attributed to wartime enemies.[102] Of course, some propaganda of the most momentary value is to be expected under such circumstances, and there can be no doubt that Noriega was a most unsavoury person with a clutch of exotic tastes.[103] However, his crimes are in no sense comparable to those of Saddam Hussein – seven civilians were killed by Panamanian security forces during the six years he commanded them – and his unfortunate dermatological condition already provided opponents with an easy enough target for abuse. Ugly, manifestly insecure and often clumsy in his political dealings, Noriega was never of such imposing stature or inscrutable demeanour that the possession of vermillion singlets might be deemed a decisive debility, even if they were donned for occult purposes.

It is, of course, the case that in Panama Washington confronted a variant of the problem that it had itself contrived to present to its opponents elsewhere in the region – how to reveal and exploit the contradictions of an authoritarian regime with a democratic façade and some space for legal opposition. However, the possibilities for opposition in Panama until 1988 were at least as great as those in Mexico, and certainly better than in Guatemala and El Salvador for the previous fifteen years. Moreover, Washington had long acquiesced in the cavalier use by both General Omar Torrijos and Noriega of 'front men' as presidents (Demetrio Lakas, 1972–78; Aristides Royo, 1978–82; Ricardo de la Espriella, 1982–84; Jorge Illueca, 1984; Nicolás Ardito Barletta, 1984–85; Erick Delvalle, 1985–88). The US raised no complaint at the fact that the May 1984 election, which Ardito Barletta formally won by less than 2,000 votes, was palpably fraudulent.[104] Neither was there any serious attempt to defend Ardito Barletta, when, in the face of his complaints at the brutal murder of leading oppositionist Hugo Spadafora, the president was ousted by Noriega in September 1985, despite the fact that this was the first Latin American coup of the Reagan administration and that Ardito Barletta was a conservative close to Washington.[105] Such acquiescence had very deep roots and was not readily reversed. When, during the course of 1986, this became inevitable, the retreat was necessarily conducted under the broadest cover of propaganda and distraction.

The fact that the problem was always presented as that of a man – Noriega – rather than a system is understandable and, indeed, partly justified, because as head of military intelligence from 1970 to 1983 and commander of the FDP since 1983 Noriega ran and represented the system in a more or less clandestine fashion. The virulence of the *ad hominem* attacks made by Washington from 1988 must, though, be related to the fact that it was revealed to have indulged Noriega's involvement in activities that were either illegal or advantageous to forces that the US government considered its foes. This was made plain by rapid but diligent journalistic investigation – subsequently vindicated by a trial that was scarcely 'fair' but amply supplied with hard evidence. Although there had been some inconclusive evidence linking Noriega to drug-dealing even as early as 1971, such activities were well known to the DEA in mid 1982, when the general established ties with the Medellín cartel, and conclusively demonstrated by mid 1986, when Noriega's pilot Floyd Carlton started to testify to US officials.[106] The DEA, however, continued to collaborate with Noriega and sent him letters congratulating him on his performance as late as May 1987. In similar vein, whilst the Carter administration immediately took Noriega off the CIA payroll, he was reinstated under Reagan even though Vice-President George Bush, as President Ford's director of the CIA in 1976, possessed first-hand knowledge of Noriega's running of agents inside the US military and his ties with Cuba. The 'realist' understanding was that Washington could control the former and benefit from the latter.[107] Equally, the fact that Torrijos and Noriega had run guns to the

Sandinistas in the late 1970s and – much more provocatively – to the Salvadorean FMLN in the 1980s was not viewed as disqualifying Noriega from overtures in 1985 by Colonel Oliver North for help in training the anti-Sandinista Contra forces.[108]

There is little challenge in criticizing the limited reward of such realpolitik or in discerning the wider damage caused by its assertively amoral presumptions. What is of greater interest for our purposes is the manner in which the US came to 'divorce' its dictator in terms of Central American politics as a whole. The first important point here is that this derived from a split in the US right between those, led by Senator Jesse Helms, who were determined to attack almost any Panamanian leader following the 1977 Canal treaty but had an excellent target anyway in Noriega, and those, such as CIA Director William Casey, who perceived the operational advantage of cooperating with Noriega as far outweighing any other consideration. Thus, in September 1986, just weeks before the Iran-Contra scandal blew up, Helms, who had been lobbied by the Spadafora family, refused to remove a relatively innocuous anti-Noriega amendment to the Intelligence Appropriations Bill.[109] Moreover, he was soon supported in this by none other than Senator John Kerry – a man of almost totally opposed beliefs – because the Democrat could see that although Helms was striving to rewrite the history of the isthmus, he had chosen to do so over an issue that had cost US liberals much support in the 1980 election and yet could now be transformed into an anti-dictatorial campaign with which progressive opinion needed to be aligned. This was particularly the case in the wake of the overthrow of Marcos in the Philippines and Duvalier in Haiti in February 1986.[110]

In June 1986 the *New York Times* had published an article by Seymour Hersh that revealed much detail on Noriega's past but did not explore the links with North and the Contras which were precisely the ones that Noriega leaked in response to the Helms amendment in September.[111] This reaction certainly advanced the revelations that so hurt the Reagan government, but it also sparked off a crisis for Noriega himself. It now seems that whilst all Central American politicians and senior military officers appreciate the divisions and cross-currents that prevail in Washington, Noriega misconstrued these and reacted against the 'right–left' alliance of Helms–Kerry–Hersh by attacking the clandestine capers of the reactionary North–Casey–Pointdexter grouping, not least perhaps because this last gentleman had travelled to Panama in December 1985 to admonish Noriega over his activities.[112] In fact, Noriega's support for the Contra cause had been distinctly tepid from the start, for although Torrijos had been closely linked to Eden Pastora, who had left the Sandinistas in 1981, Noriega had naturally tighter ties with the Nicaraguan intelligence chief Tomás Borge, who was one of the strongest figures in the Sandinista regime and also friendly with Cuba.[113] Henceforth, Noriega would be much more closely associated with Managua and Havana than with the counter-revolutionaries, and this, together with anti-oligarchic rabble-rousing, gave his government a leftist tint over its final two years. Washington suddenly found itself with a second opponent in the region as the image of Torrijos was revived.

As Table 1 shows clearly, the Reagan administration was unable to solve the Noriega problem in short order. Indeed, during Reagan's last year in office Noriega not only survived extraordinary economic pressure, strike movements, attempted coups and a most clumsily applied carrot-and-stick policy on Washington's part; he even appeared to have fortified his position.[114] This was achieved in no small part by maintaining formal democratic activity and holding the elections scheduled for May 1989. Here we might note a parallel with the experience of Nicaragua, from which Noriega distracted much unwanted US attention during the first eighteen months after the Esquipulas accord. In both cases US pressure and the deployment of surrogate forces failed to shift an unfriendly regime and reflected poorly on Washington's authority within its own sphere of influence. Indeed, on the eve of his departure from office, Reagan threatened that the US would renege on the Canal treaty if Noriega didn't quit – a reminder that whilst he had won the 1980 election in no small measure by attacking Carter's weakness over Nicaragua and Iran, he had previously campaigned even more vehemently against the treaty signed with Torrijos in 1977.

When Bush came to office in late January 1989, Panama was the regional state over which the new president could least afford to be flexible, both because of his own past associations with Noriega and because the existence of the Canal introduced 'supra-ideological' factors where compromise was inadmissible. Nonetheless, it is perfectly possible that had Noriega permitted the opposition to win the May 1989 poll, a rapprochement of the type proposed several times over the previous year could have been secured, even though the February 1988 Grand Jury indictment was always going to make this embarrassing. By May 1989, however, the logic of dictatorship had tightened, and by October both local conditions – the Giroldi coup attempt – and the rapidly shifting international scenario – near-warfare between the state and the Medellín cartel in Colombia; the rapid collapse of the Soviet bloc – made intervention both necessary and a compelling option for the

Table 1 The Crisis in Panama, 1987–89

1987

June	1	FDP High Command announces retirement of Col. Roberto Díaz Herrera, second-in-command.
	5	Díaz accuses Noriega of rigging 1984 poll and ordering murder of Dr Hugo Spadafora in 1985; riots; constitution suspended.
	9	Establishment of business-led National Civic Crusade (CCN) opposition movement.
	26	US Senate resolution calls for Noriega to stand down and for new elections; US embassy attacked.
	29	Commercial and school strikes against Noriega called by CCN.
July	1	OAS resolution call on US to cease interference in internal Panamanian affairs, as guaranteed under 1977 Canal treaties.
	27	Col. Díaz arrested after assault on his house; formally retracts charges.
Aug.	8	US military and economic aid suspended.
	31	Anti-Noriega strike movement fizzles out.

1988

Feb.	5	US Grand Jury, Florida, indicts Noriega on narcotics and racketeering charges; State Department not previously informed.
	10	José Blandón, former consul in New York, gives detailed testimony against Noriega to US Senate sub-committee. According to Assistant Secretary of State Elliott Abrams, Noriega is 'clinging to power by his fingertips'.
	26	After talks with US, Pres. Erick Delvalle tries to remove Noriega as FDP commander and is himself promptly deposed; National Assembly appoints Manuel Solís Palma in his stead, but US continues to recognize only Delvalle as legal head of state.
March	11	US withholds payments to Canal Commission and freezes assets of Panamanian state in USA.
	16	News of abortive police coup provokes anti-Noriega riots and two-week general strike; FDP purged.
	19	State of emergency declared; banks closed (for nine weeks); 'Dignity Battalions' formed by Noriega, who holds secret talks with US envoys.
	20	US Secretary of State Shultz publicly urges Noriega to go into exile.
	22	Noriega offers to resign but insists upon choosing his own time.
April	1	Anti-Noriega strikes fizzle out.
	5	1,300 US troops sent to bolster 10,000-strong Canal garrison.
	8	Reagan uses 1977 Emergency Powers Act to impose economic sanctions.
	24	Solís appoints leftist cabinet; Church requests end to US sanctions.
	27	US disowns plans to oust Noriega and suggests compromise.
May	9	Banks re-open; State Department official Michael Kozak holds secret talks with Noriega, offering to drop charges if he leaves country.
July	27	Reagan declares that covert destabilization of Noriega regime has been authorized; CIA plan to stage coup blocked by US Senate Intelligence sub-committee out of fear that it would involve Noriega's murder.
Sept.	15	Miami judge restricts information on charges against Noriega during US election campaign.

Table 1 continued

1989		
Jan.	3	Encouraged by Washington, CCN decides to contest May elections.
	19	Reagan threatens to renege on 1977 treaty if Noriega remains in power.
May	7	Elections; widespread allegations of fraud to deny victory to ADOC candidate Guillermo Endara; protests repressed.
	10	Electoral tribunal annuls election results on grounds of public disorder and irregularities.
	11	2,000 US troops sent to Canal Zone.
	14	Pres. Bush declares that the FDP should 'do everything they can to get Mr Noriega out of there ... I would add no words of caution'.
	17	OAS foreign ministers condemn election fraud and send investigative mission; opposition strike collapses.
Aug.	16	Extensive US manoeuvres in Canal Zone.
	31	Council of State dissolves National Assembly and names provisional government headed by ex-Attorney General Francisco Rodríguez; OAS mediation abandoned.
Oct.	2	Gen. Maxwell Thurman named new head of US Southcom.
	3	Coup attempt by Major Moisés Giroldi fails; US forces provide only limited support; Giroldi and others executed.
Dec.	15	National Assembly declares war on USA and names Noriega 'maximum leader'.
	20	24,000 US troops invade in 'Operation Just Cause'.
	24	Noriega seeks asylum in Papal nunciature.
1990		
Jan.	3	Noriega surrenders to US forces, is shipped to Miami and indicted on drugs charges.

US administration. Noriega, then, acted as a lightning-rod for the Bush government at a crucial moment in the negotiations between Managua and the Contras and just as the FMLN were preparing their offensive on San Salvador. In one sense Panama 'became' part of Central America, and in another it served as a proximate distraction.

Both senses seem likely to remain valid, and not only because the important anomalies in Panama's status as a nation-state derived from the Canal will persist until the end of the century. In geo-political terms Panama has been brought much closer to the rest of the region by the 1989 invasion and the subsequent reconstitution of its domestic affairs on terms comparable to those elsewhere. Similar problems exist, for instance, in terms of tense civil–military relations, the very fragile rule of law, and diminished ideological appeal on both the right – widely viewed as white-skinned sepoys of the *gringos* – and the left, which frittered away much of the political potential provided by US control of the Canal in supporting the distinctly fair-weather 'bonapartism' of Noriega as well as Torrijos. This might work to the benefit of a quite unusual force in Rubén Blades's movement Papa Egoró – a popular formation that could only be nationalist and simultaneously exhibit strong pan-Caribbean features by virtue of being Panamanian. Equally, Panama's peculiar economic position cannot readily be adjusted to those of the CACM/CEC states because of the key role of its banks. Perhaps most important of all, Panama's role in drug-trafficking has evidently not diminished since the invasion, placing it to the fore of what was for most of the Bush presidency a core issue in US domestic and foreign policy.

Drugs and Corruption

The National Drug Control Strategy launched on US television by President Bush in September 1989 had the Andean countries of Colombia, Peru and Bolivia as its key Latin American targets. Even though the Berlin Wall was still in place when Bush made his address, one can discern the movement in US priorities in the increase of Washington's military aid to these coca/cocaine-producing countries from $81.5 million ($73 million to Colombia) in 1989 to $142.2 million in 1990 (with $141.3 million requested for 1991) when that to Central America was being reduced from $132 million to $107 million.[115] However, just as Washington leaned heavily on a counter-insurgency mentality and the image of 'narco-guerrillas' for its Andean strategy, so too, in a curious inversion, did a 'decommunized' Central America present a muddled picture with a clear expansion of drug production, smuggling and even consumption in the early 1990s.[116]

Panama, as has been indicated, remained exceptional, even by the standards of Latin America as a whole. According to some sources the trade in cocaine rose fourfold between 1990 and 1992. Seizures in this period amounted to 29,000 kilos, the courts identified 85 per cent of all arrests as being related to narcotics, and the country's 'historic' role of laundering Colombian 'narcodollars' seems to have been maintained without great inconvenience.[117] Judging by the distinctly clumsy – but at least partly reliable – indicators for seizures of cocaine, Panama accounted for more activity than the rest of Central America combined, with 18,700 kilos in 1992.[118] Nevertheless, the increase elsewhere is notable, Guatemala becoming the world's third-largest producer of opium (valued at $1.5 billion in 1989) with significant trade in marijuana ($38 million a year) and cocaine ($192 million) even before the installation of the powerful US radar station at Trujillo (Honduras) enhanced the importance of many of the country's 1,000 airstrips by more effectively scanning the Caribbean approaches to the USA.[119] The DEA has been operating in Guatemala since 1986, not just to stage local operations – 3.7 tons of cocaine were seized in the first nine months of 1991 – but also to coordinate those in El Salvador (3,000 kilos seized in Acajutla in October 1991), Honduras (amongst several cases the mistaken arrest by FUSEP of a DEA plant on a 'sting' in April 1991), and Costa Rica (the large joint 'Operación Talamanca' of June 1990).[120] The rise in drug-related activity in Nicaragua may be attributed to the influence of exiles returning from Miami, the lifting of tight economic controls in general, or the repatriation of Contra enterprise, but as elsewhere it must also be explained in terms of Central America's location between the main production centres and the USA. This, together with the sharp increase of controls on the Mexican border, has made the region a natural entrepot.

It has been said of Noriega that 'drugs didn't corrupt [him]; rather corruption led him to the drug dealers'.[121] This is only partially true elsewhere, and there have been some notable cases of suspected smugglers being released by judges without outwardly persuasive cause. According to the Honduran Commission Against Drug Trafficking, 98 per cent of the suspects held in 800 cases in 1991 were set free by police or judges.[122] In a similar vein, General Humberto Regalado was effectively vetoed by Washington from re-election as commander of the armed forces by revelation of accusations of embezzling US aid in October 1989, after he had avoided charges for trafficking drugs in 1988.[123] Regalado's general political vulnerability was increased by the implication of several members of his family in drug-smuggling. This was also true of Guatemalan President Vinicio Cerezo, whose brother Milton was arrested for trading in dope and passports in March 1990, as had been Carlos Cabrera, brother of Vice-President Alfonso Cabrera, whose candidacy on behalf of the Christian Democrats in the 1991 elections was greatly weakened by this association, although he was never a strong contender.[124] In both these instances the US took a very public interest in the charges. By contrast, Washington's intervention in the extended and highly politicized scandal surrounding ex-President Daniel Oduber of Costa Rica over his alleged receipt of campaign funds from US smuggler Lionel Casey – together with similar allegations made against Presidents Monge, Arias and Calderón – was conspicuous by its absence, perhaps because the accusations touched on Contra activities and US companies.[125] In all events, Costa Rican politics have in recent years become prey to such charges although (or possibly because) legislative investigation has been markedly more efficient than else-where, not least, as Christopher Hitchens has wryly remarked, by declaring Colonel Oliver North, General Richard Secord, Admiral John Pointdexter, Ambassador Lewis Tambs, and former San José CIA chief Joseph Fernández *personae non gratae* for illegal activities conducive to drug-smuggling.[126]

The exploitation of Costa Rica for asylum, money-laundering and relatively cheap pay-offs may have been the result of the country's solitary openness throughout the 1980s as well as its proximity to Panama. One should, though, be cautious in attributing to constitutional regimes a greater tendency to corruption when this may merely be broader in its reach and more readily publicized than under dictatorships. Moreover, there are a number of signs that reactions to and disputes over questionable conduct by public figures matter more in Central American politics than for many years. In El Salvador the Christian Democrat (PDC) victory in the 1985 legislative elections followed intensive publicity given by the party to the detention in Corpus Christi, Texas, of Francisco Guirola, a close friend of Roberto D'Aubuissón who was caught attempting to smuggle $5.8 million out of the US to fund the ARENA campaign.[127] However, the PDC's tightened control of government resulted in extensive accusations of corruption against them, despite the fact that President Duarte pointedly refused to allow the state to take responsibility for international assistance provided after the 1986 earthquake. Two factions developed within the party – and eventually split it – over the issues of personalism, malfeasance and lack of accountability. ARENA easily won the 1988 legislative elections, which it had contested on a platform that stressed the PDC's corruption almost as much as the need for neo-liberal reforms. Subsequently a congressional commission investigated charges against fifteen members of the PDC (and three from ARENA) alleged to have stolen $43 million from public coffers, USAID, and funds destined for the Contras.[128] Following ARENA's capture of the presidency in 1989, Duarte himself was obliged to answer charges that he had misused 500,000 Colones donated for earthquake relief.[129] To some degree the tables were turned once again in the autumn of 1992 when the government felt obliged to set up a new commission after the arrest of Heriberto Guerrero, director of the National Commission for Attention to the Displaced (CONADES), for malfeasance, and the existence of strong evidence of wrongdoing in the Supreme Court and the Rio Lempa Power Company (CEL).[130]

In Guatemala, as we will see, non-drug-related corruption was a key component in eroding the authority of the Serrano regime, dissolving the alliances upon which its survival depended, and sparking off the 1993 crisis. Equally, whilst the Sandinistas had for more than a decade resisted a formidable US propaganda offensive by dint of impressive ethical conduct in government, the reputation of the party leadership was only enhanced amongst the most diehard FSLN supporters by the awarding, after the electoral defeat, of expropriated houses to those – principally Sandinistas – living in them on the day of the poll. Coming as part of a rapidly approved legal package – Laws 85, 86 and 88 – that consolidated some 15,000 agrarian reform and other property titles, this measure was projected as part of a general effort to complete and protect the social gains of the 1979 Revolution. However, it was almost immediately dubbed the *piñata* – a doll filled with sweets to be burst open at children's parties – by the conservative press, and this image stuck. For some, such as Humberto Ortega, it was an overdue and justified retreat from idealism.[131] For others, like his brother Daniel, the measure was initially defensible as a defiant 'last blast', whilst Comandante Bayardo Arce noted that the FSLN had previously donated 'its' property to the state.[132] None of these presentations convinced a large sector of the Sandinista rank and file that the property seizures had improved the party's credibility – not least when Daniel Ortega's own large house was part of the deal – and the FSLN's conference at El Crucero in June 1990 produced both criticism – led by the prominent militant Rafael Solís – and the establishment of a commission to investigate corruption amongst party officials and leaders.[133] The *piñata* may perhaps be best seen as an expression of FSLN hubris insofar as the party had made no serious provision for defeat at the polls and had, therefore, to rush through compensatory measures that could otherwise have been implemented in a much more presentable manner.

The experience of Honduras could not be more different in that it has become positively characteristic of the political system that senior public figures extend irregular commerce in posts and influence to irregular commerce in debt, lumber, coffee, cattle and precious stones.[134] If the presence of the Contras – in significant numbers from 1983 to 1990 – provided some quite tough competition in terms of both contraband and access to US sources, the increased leverage this gave in bargaining with Washington provided appreciable compensation, as did the considerable 'spill-overs' and natural market distribution of US aid to the Nicaraguan counter-revolutionaries.[135] However, neither the windfall gains gleaned through the Contras nor the tensions caused by these greatly affected the traditional two-party system. After the 1985 poll one key mechanism through which this accommodated a variety of clientelist networks shifted from a multi-candidate party slate to the holding of primaries – a development that arguably increased the focus – if not the level – of muck-raking since only the Liberals held genuine contests in 1988 and 1993. The 1989 campaign was marked by constant PN claims that the Liberals were funding their candidate Carlos Flores from state funds; the substantiated allegation by the Liberal daily *Tiempo* that leading PN figure Osmond Maduro had illegally received $7 million at preferential exchange rates from the Central Bank, then presided over by his brother Ricardo; and the no less persuasive charges, from the minority PINU and Christian Democrat parties, that $6.5 million of USAID funds paid to the North American firm Dual Associated to draw up a reasonably respectable electoral register had been – after three failed attempts – not only wasted but probably also spent to pad out the rolls.[136] One other notable feature of Honduran politics in recent years has been the extremely flexible interpretation of constitutional ordinances with regard to high judicial office. Prior to the multi-candidate 1985 poll the Liberals had come badly unstuck over attempted congressional manipulation of the membership and powers of the Supreme Court by one faction of the party.[137] In September 1991 the extreme right-wing PN leader Oswaldo Ramos Soto was removed by Congress as president of the Supreme Court for using it as a political platform in support of his campaign to become party candidate in the 1993 presidential poll. Early in that year Ramos Soto finally achieved his ambition – without any formal contest – only for the PN members of Congress to remove their co-religionist Leonardo Matute Murillo as Attorney General in May because, it was claimed, the constitution prohibited him from simultaneously serving in the Central American Parliament (PARLACEN). This was despite the fact that Matute had threatened corruption charges against those deputies who voted to remove him.[138] The Liberals abstained from the vote, claiming that the PN was conducting its internal politics through the offices of the state, which at least had the merit of manifesting some transparency.

Esquipulas

By its very nature diplomacy is complicated and generally difficult to follow. This is certainly the case in the still-partial settlement of the Central American conflict, but a few broad observations may still usefully be made. Perhaps the most obvious and important is that the various negotiations – but particularly those known as Esquipulas II – represented a significant setback for 'realism' or 'geographical fatalism', broadly understood as the acceptance of a static balance of forces and projection of optimum US armed capacity and influence as realpoli-tik.[139] It is clearly not the case, however, that every phase of the settlement was achieved in the face of US opposition. We can contrast the nature of the Salvadorean negotiations of 1990–91 – when an essentially domestic treaty was brokered internationally and depended heavily upon Washington's conditional withdrawal of funds – with those for Nicaragua in 1987–89, which took the form of an inter-national treaty that possessed important domestic implications, required direct internal agreements for its success, and was forced through with great difficulty since Washington (not a signatory) maintained funds to the rebels in open defiance of one of the treaty's core clauses. Nonetheless, the experience of the fiercely contested Nicaraguan settlement was in itself a factor in shifting the Bush administration's approach after 1990, not least because it had revealed the difficulties of sustaining an overt but informal international alliance against a protagonist that was far more flexible than had been anticipated. It was not, then, just the collapse of the Berlin Wall or the replacement of Reagan that permitted the region's main civil wars to be halted; the diplomacy had acquired a momentum of its own.

The details of the Nicaraguan negotiations that lay at the heart of the Esquipulas process are laid out in Table 2. Whilst some on the left interpret this trajectory as one of virtually unconditional surrender by the FSLN, others have argued that it demonstrates considerable dexterity in the absence of any viable alternative.[140] As has already been mentioned, diplomacy is scarcely heroic in the most tranquil of seasons, and it can easily appear cynical and capitulationist when conducted simultaneously with fierce fighting and acute human suffering. In the case of Central America, moreover, diplomacy had been seen through most of the 1980s as a futile activity because of the Reagan administra-tion's effective veto of any serious negotiations with the Sandinistas or the Salvadorean rebels. This, it might be recalled, contrasted with the approach of the Carter government, which in 1979 tried to resolve the Sandinista-led insurrection against Somoza precisely through mediation by an Organization of American States (OAS) peace-keeping force. The Reagan shift was hardened by the Franco-Mexican recognition in September 1981 of the FMLN as a representative political force and the renewed Mexican effort in February 1982 to initiate talks on Cuba as well as Nicaragua and El Salvador.[141] Nevertheless, the White House was obliged at least formally to address the initiatives opened early in January 1983 by the foreign ministers of Mexico, Colombia, Venezuela and Panama on the Panamanian island of Contadora, which subse-quently lent its name to this group.

Table 2   The Central American Settlement: Esquipulas and Nicaragua

1986	May	Esquipulas, Guatemala: presidential summit convened by Cerezo stalls after Arias–Ortega argument over democracy; Contadora draft rejected by Costa Rica, El Salvador, Honduras.
1987	Feb.	San José, Costa Rica: Arias calls presidential summit (excluding Ortega) to discuss plan balancing requirements for internal democratization with ending of external support for rebels; this drops Contadora's focus on foreign bases, inter-state relations and formal sovereignty. Duarte and Ortega soon reverse their immediate rejection.
	June	Washington DC, USA: Arias visits Reagan, who criticizes plan for indulging Nicaragua.
	July	Tegucigalpa, Honduras: twice-delayed presidential summit presented with entirely new draft proposals; these withdrawn after Mexico pressures Hondurans; Arias proposals retabled; agreed that ceasefires be between governments and rebels; 'suspension of military aid' to rebels becomes 'cessation of all aid', except for repatriation and resettlement.
	Aug.	Washington: Reagan and Speaker Wright announce plan (5th) for sixty-day Contra ceasefire but with rebels to continue receiving US aid. Esquipulas: presidents sign (7th) Arias plan as amended in July – known as 'Esquipulas II'; Wright supports this accord, which calls for five actions within ninety days: (i) amnesty for irregular forces (who are to release their prisoners); (ii) ceasefire; (iii) promotion of pluralist democracy with freedoms of expression and association; (iv) cessation of all aid to rebel forces, except for repatriation and relocation; (v) prevention of use of territory by rebel forces attacking other states.
	Nov.	Managua, Nicaragua (5th): Ortega reverses five-year policy and announces indirect talks with Contras.
1988	Jan.	Alajuela, Costa Rica (16th–21st): presidential summit calls on USA to halt funding of Contras, for whom Reagan administration has requested $270 million from Congress; Ortega accepts lack of statement on role of Honduras, contravening clause on use of territory.
	Feb.	Washington (3rd): House rejects reduced administration request of $36 million for Contras by a margin of eight votes.
	March	Sapoá, Nicaragua (21st): government–Contra ceasefire for sixty days from 1 April whilst Contra troops relocate; many Contra prisoners amnestied; Contras permitted to join National Dialogue and political parties.
	April	Managua (17th): government proposes permanent ceasefire, rejected by Contras, but Alfredo César, rebel political leader, continues secret talks.
	May	Managua (26th–28th): government accepts direct talks on political conditions with Contras; César backs off.

Table 2 continued

	June	Managua (9th): Contras demand right of conscripts to leave army when they choose, resignation of entire Supreme Court, and return of confiscated property whilst they retain arms until Jan. 1989; government rejects demands and reveals talks with César; Contras walk out.
1989	Feb.	Caracas, Venezuela (2nd): regional presidents (bar ailing Duarte) meet at inauguration of Carlos Andrés Pérez; Ortega agrees, with Castro's approval, to open elections, international observers and reform of electoral law in exchange for pressure over Contras from other states. Tesoro Beach, El Salvador (15th): presidential summit requests foreign ministers to liaise with UN over implementation of Esquipulas II within ninety days; Contras to be resettled under multilateral agreement, not bilateral accord between Nicaragua and Honduras; opposition to all aid to Contras reiterated; Nicaragua agrees to advance poll to Feb. 1990. Washington (16th and 24th): Bush and Quayle cast doubt on Tesoro Beach agreements and reiterate support for Contras.
	March	Washington (24th): Bush announces agreement with Congress to provide Contras with aid until Nicaraguan elections as guarantee; Honduras requested to leave Contras unmolested; Esquipulas framework tacitly accepted on all other points.
	April	Managua (18th): electoral law reformed to enfranchise those who boycotted 1984 poll; surprised parliamentary opposition claims this insufficient and walks out; US and regional governments cast doubt on FSLN motives.
	July	San José (14th): at meeting with Arias, Ortega agrees to meet opposition collectively.
	Aug.	Managua (3rd and 4th): Ortega holds twenty-two-hour televised meeting with twenty opposition parties, which agree to participate in 1990 poll. Tela, Honduras (5th–7th): presidential summit agrees disbanding of Contra forces by 5th December and calls on OAS and UN to establish bodies to observe (ONUCA) process and organize demobilization (CIAV); Bush dismisses deadline but offers formal support; Nicaragua drops case against Honduras in World Court.
	Oct.	Managua (21st): re-infiltrating Contras kill eighteen reservists; Ortega cancels unilateral ceasefire to draw attention to continued clashes; US Senate votes 95–0 in condemnation of this.
	Nov.	New York and Washington (9th–21st): CIAV convenes Managua–Contra talks; government accepts evacuation of only those Contra troops infiltrated since Tela agreement; Contras refuse to withdraw any forces.
	Dec.	San Isidro de Coronado, Costa Rica (10th–12th): emergency presidential summit following rebel offensive in El Salvador; Ortega joins condemnation in order to gain support against Contras and agreement to demand that Contra aid is handed to CIAV; ONUCA mandate extended.

The Contadora proposals, which first took form after a meeting of the group at Cancún in July 1983, rested on the laudable but then quite impracticable premisses on the one hand of the principle of equality of states, sovereignty and self-determination, and on the other that adherence to international rules of peaceful coexistence is infectious. Eschewing any direct attention to internal political matters – Mexico had fiercely resisted this over Nicaragua in 1979 – the Contadora group concentrated on control of arms supplies; removal of foreign advisers; creation of demilitarized zones; prohibition of activities destabilizing neighbouring countries; and prohibition of any political or military intervention in another state.[142] A list of twenty-one proposals to these ends was formally presented to the region's foreign ministers in June 1984 together with a draft Act of Peace and Cooperation. However, only the Guatemalan and Nicaraguan governments reacted favourably; and by November only Managua declared that it would sign whilst Costa Rica, El Salvador and Honduras demanded more guarantees of Nicaraguan compliance, in line with Washington's view that Managua itself was the cause of the conflict.

This alignment patently challenged the Contadora initiative, which now seemed destined to decompose into a forum where the regional allies of the US could eternally amend worthy proposals without exercising any influence over the fighting. The US invasion of Grenada in October 1983 gave force to the almost flippant opinion of the Kissinger Report, issued in January 1984, that 'the interests of the four Contadora countries are not identical, nor coincidental to those of the United States, and hence the United States cannot use the Contadora process as a substitute for its policies'.[143]

On the other hand, Contadora's identification of extra-regional provocation as a major element in the conflict between Central American states was in keeping with the shift in Latin American political temper in the mid 1980s, and a support group comprising Brazil, Argentina, Uruguay and Peru was established in July 1985 to give the initiative some renewed energy. This certainly required Washington to take seriously the hitherto underemphasized diplomatic side of its 'dual track' offensive against the Sandinistas, but it is perhaps unsurprising that the augmented group achieved little beyond ringing declarations when Washington's surrogate war was achieving tangible results, thereby obviating the need for the direct intervention that preoccupied continental diplomats.[144]

The shift in this scenario took place in 1986, with the election of Vinicio Cerezo, never a close Washington ally and so able to operate more independently, as president of Guatemala, and Oscar Arias, emphatically a US friend and so able to grasp the importance of that element – internal political conditionality – that was scrupulously omitted from the Contadora proposals and yet would be crucial to Washington if it should have to settle for less than the complete annihilation of the FSLN, as president of Costa Rica. The possibility of such an eventuality was, of course, greatly increased with the breaking of the Iran-Contra scandal in November 1986, four months after the first meeting at Esquipulas which had closed acrimoniously because Arias had maintained Costa Rica's record of being the neighbour most openly critical of Nicaragua.[145]

The Arias proposals of February 1987 shifted the diplomatic focus from inter-state relations to establishing a linkage between greater internal reform and reduced external intervention. This change initially surprised and alienated Managua – which had been excluded from the meeting – as well as Washington and its local allies. However, the fact that it emanated from a state friendly to the US, as well as echoing much of the rhetoric of conditionality employed by the Reagan administration in its negotiations over Contra funding with Congress, meant that the proposal could not be dismissed as readily as had been Contadora. Furthermore, the Iran-Contra scandal opened a critical fissure in the White House's relations with a Congress angry at having been cheated of its fiscal power in a matter that related to Central America. This much-televised rupture provided the governments of the isthmus with the unprecedented option of shifting diplomatic position and tentatively constructing a regional bloc whilst still retaining some support in Washington. The option, though, could only be properly realized in the detail – as a treaty was haggled over for real rather than simply postponed *sine die* at the behest of the US.

That process began in earnest on 7 August 1987, after two final efforts to sabotage the initiative – in Tegucigalpa the previous month, when Mexico prevented the bullied Hondurans from replacing the Arias draft entirely; and in Washington itself on 5 August, when House Speaker Jim Wright momentarily backed Reagan in trying to pre-empt the Central American accord with a poorly designed alternative that sought to give the impression of serious US concessions but offered many less than required by the Arias draft. Under such circumstances the mere fact that the Esquipulas II accord was signed is perhaps a more important achievement than for many other international treaties where signature bears a relatively low cost. However, as can be seen from Table 2, implementation was a sharply contested process in which Washington never surrendered its use of the Contras as security and a bargaining chip for successive Sandinista concessions, which were often made against US expectations and to the bewilderment of a Contra leadership disoriented by insecurity to its rear in Washington and before it in Managua.

Nicaragua lay at the heart of the Esquipulas process because its civil war had largely been generated by the USA and directly affected two further states (Costa Rica and Honduras). Equally, of course, the fact that Washington's opponents in Nicaragua controlled the national government meant that they could more easily enter into an international treaty. As we will see, the position in El Salvador was quite different although undoubtedly influenced by the precedent established over Nicaragua as well as the broad framework given by Esquipulas.

Refuge, Relocation and Return

The experience of refuge is not new to Central America, but never – even at the time of the Spanish conquest – has it affected so many people as during the 1980s.[146] Most of the figures in Table 3 are estimates, but even if we allow generous margins of error the impact of the regional civil wars and economic crisis is abundantly clear. Perhaps 5 per cent of the isthmian population perforce moved its place of residence between 1978 and 1993. With that movement those people underwent experiences far more exigent – and generally traumatic – than those inferred by simple resettlement. Whether such movement entailed exile in a foreign country or not, it meant unsought departure from familiar surroundings and sources of economic and emotional support. In most cases this has been the result of fear of violence by military forces. In Guatemala, particularly, it has derived from a clear and detailed strategy by the army to destroy rural settlements and relocate their populations in strategic hamlets under its control. In other cases – notably in the USA – we might speak of 'economic refugees', but the 'push factor' is often far more complex and nasty than simple privation.

The scale of the refugee experience in Central America outstrips that of South America a decade earlier, when the victims of dictatorship mostly went into foreign exile. Moreover, Southern Cone refugees were – with the possible exception of Uruguay – generally identifiable political opponents of the authoritarian regimes driving them out, rather than people 'in the way' of operations or occupants of combat or free-fire zones, which correspond much more to the rural and directly contested conflicts in the isthmus. In Guatemala, El Salvador and, to a lesser degree, the Atlantic coast of Nicaragua, the state's army often identified entire communities as 'subversive', dealing with them

Table 3 Central American Refugees and Displaced Persons, 1987 and 1990[1]

(i) 1987	Salvadoreans	Guatemalans	Hondurans	Nicaraguans	Total
Internally displaced	500,000	100,000– 200,000	35,000	250,000	885,000– 985,000
Refugees					
in Panama	900	NA	NA	300	1,200
in Costa Rica	6,200	200	NA	22,000– 100,000	28,400– 106,400
in Nicaragua	7,600	500	NA	—	8,100
in Honduras	24,000	1,000	—	43,000	68,000
in El Salvador	—	NA	NA	400	400
in Guatemala	10,000	—	NA	2,000– 20,000	12,000– 30,000
in Mexico	120,000– 250,000	45,000– 150,000	NA	NA	165,000– 400,000
in USA	500,000– 800,000	100,000– 200,000	50,000– 100,000	40,000– 80,000	690,000– 1,180,000
in Canada	4,600	485	NA	NA	5,085
in Australia	600	NA	NA	NA	600
in Belize	3,000	6,000	NA	NA	9,000
Total	1,176,900– 1,606,900	253,185– 558,185	85,000– 135,000	357,700– 493,700	1,872,785– 2,843,785

(ii) 1990	Salvadoreans	Guatemalans	Nicaraguans	Undocumented
Refugees				
in Belize	3,000	6,000	NA	25,000
in Costa Rica	NA	NA	46,000	150,000– 175,000
in El Salvador	—	NA	630	3,000– 5,000
in Guatemala	2,800	—	3,200	200,000
in Honduras	2,800	450	23,000	200,000
in Mexico	NA	40,500	NA	300,000
Official repatriates (Jan. 1984– Mar. 1990)	30,000	5,600	30,000– 35,000	—
Internally displaced	134,000– 400,000	100,000– 250,000	350,000	—
Total Refugees	87,800	47,450	72,200	875,000– 900,000

Note: 1. All figures given are estimates, either of governments or of international bodies. Different figures given represent the spread of serious estimates. Full explanations are given in the sources: for 1987 – Patricia Weiss Fagen, 'Central American Refugees and US Policy', in Nora Hamilton *et al.*, eds., *Crisis in Central America*, Boulder 1988, pp. 75–6; for 1990 – CAR, 13 July 1990. Comparable figures are given in CEPAL, *El Impacto Económico y Social de las Migraciones en Centroamérica*, Santiago de Chile 1993.

en masse. One consequence of this has been refuge by community group, often across national borders to camps – mostly in Mexico and Honduras – run by the United Nations High Commission for Refugees (UNHCR). Government conviction that these communities are important political bodies – if not direct puppets of the rebels – is evident in their marked reluctance to permit resettlement on any but their own terms.

In the case of Guatemala it took two years of negotiations before an agreement was finally reached in October 1992 for the return of 43,000 refugees in camps in Mexico – a decade after the start of the counter-insurgency operations that had driven these people from their predominantly highland homes. Until this agreement fewer than 8,000 of the estimated 150,000 external refugees had returned over five years, most of them to a few villages in Huehuetenango.[147] The October 1992 accord between the state and the refugees' organization (CCPP) may be seen as indicative of both the form and the substance of the transitional period of Central American politics as new organizations negotiate preliminary rights for constituencies in limbo. In this case the CCPP secured state agreement to treat the returnees as civilians – no small achievement even under the tempered counter-insurgency mentality prevailing within the military – and exempt from service in both the military and the civil patrols that had been so integral to military control in the countryside. Land and credit were promised, and implementation was subject to oversight and guarantees by the Church, the UN and the national ombudsman for human rights. In August 1992, before such conditions could be secured, over 1,000 refugees who had re-entered the country on their own after ten years in Mexico were obliged to return there.[148] In the autumn of 1992 Rigoberta Menchú and other popular leaders publicly advised against return on the grounds of insufficient guarantees, thereby drawing attention to the importance of this issue to the reconstitution of civil society and the establishment of the preconditions of citizenship.

In a rather different vein, Richard Wilson has argued eloquently that it is mistaken to view the state – and especially the army – as simply 'alien' in highland Guatemala. At least with respect to the Q'eqchi' villages he has studied it is more than this, insinuating itself within the community and manipulating traditional customs and practices for political ends. As a consequence, the experience of violent upheaval and forced relocation under uncertain terms has been especially complex and noxious. Even very localized religious beliefs focused on mountain spirits have been prey to manipulation, and, of course, these are extremely difficult to sustain when communities are forcibly removed from their traditional – and thus sacred – homes.[149] Yet here too one observes an exceptional resilience that should be weighed against the hardships endured by both internal and external refugees. Perhaps the most impressive examples of this are the Communities of Populations in Resistance (CPRs) representing perhaps 15,000 people who have been living an almost completely clandestine existence in northern Quiché for the better part of a decade. Many more people in the countryside have adopted a semi-nomadic life, fleeing the presence of the army in a manner similar to the *guindas* undertaken by communities in the combat zones of northern and eastern El Salvador in the mid 1980s. All the evidence is that senior military commanders – particularly in Guatemala – are more aware than the politicians that the experience of these groups has altered their identity in a manner that is only partially recognizable in terms of orthodox European ideologies.

The scale of repatriation and resettlement is not fully evident from Table 3 because it occurred largely after 1990. Moreover, the ending of hostilities has been neither a necessary nor a sufficient condition for return. Costa Rica, which has itself created no exiles to speak of, has some 100,000 undocumented inhabitants in large measure because of the parlous state of the Nicaraguan economy.[150] On the other hand, El Salvador witnessed a significant flow of mass repatriations before the final ceasefire and in many cases against government instructions. Salvadorean resettlement began tentatively in October 1987, in the wake of Esquipulas, involving some 7,500 people over the following year and 27,000 by 1991.[151] By early 1992 almost all Salvadorean refugee camps had been closed, but by the same token some 200,000 people in the country lacked official documentation, which, apart from complicating many aspects of life in a traditionally bureaucratic society, posed questions as to their ability to participate in formal political life. Nevertheless, both the flow and the initiative of returning Salvadorean refugees may be identified as key factors in the process of pacification, notwithstanding the sometimes sharp clashes over the place, timing and form of repatriation. Perhaps the most prominent example in this respect is the establishment of Ciudad Segundo Montes in the department of Morazán, where refugees returning from camps in Honduras founded a community that was embattled and somewhat artificial in its foreign funding but also possessed of exemplary qualities in the organization of health, education and economy. Just as important was the exceptional manner in which Segundo Montes straddled the formal and informal states administered by the San Salvador government and the FMLN, providing a momentarily famous illustration of changes in outlook and conduct that were normally expressed in more surreptitious, even subterranean, manner. The point here is less that hundreds of thousands of people have been radicalized by being uprooted and subjected to duress for the better part of a dozen years; it is, rather, that such affiliations have not simply been neutralized by resettlement. It is not sensible to suppose that relocation will simply permit a spatially re-ordered return to the *status quo ante*, except, perhaps, in the case of Honduras, which has a substantially reduced refugee problem – largely managed and funded by the US and the UN – and so few exiles of its own that their return in the spring of 1991 made no economic and minimal political impact.[152]

In Nicaragua many of those displaced by the war themselves participated in it as combatants. Their response to the failure of the Chamorro government to provide the land and credit promised from April 1990 onwards was, not unnaturally, renewed recourse to violence. Here the problems of military demobilization overlap substantially with those of resettlement and 'integration' – perhaps a perverse term to be used in this context given that Contra and Sandinista troops were at the heart of national politics during the 1980s. As so often in such cases, there has been much exploitation of volatile conditions in order to engage in simple banditry, which has a long history in Nicaragua. Nonetheless, restitution of public order through 'exemplary' repression of the type meted out by the EPS against its own ex-comrades in Estelí in July 1993 is likely to yield a strictly Pyrrhic victory unless backed by finite concessions to demands of widely acknowledged reasonableness.

The problem – predictably – has been that of funding resettlement programmes at a time of sharp economic recession. Moreover, erstwhile US largesse towards military supplicants was not only reduced by operational redundancy and formidable competition from elsewhere in the world; it was also succeeded by a new phase of congressionally driven conditionality. This was most tightly counter-productive and vindictive in the case of Nicaragua, where by mid 1993 the position had become sufficiently severe for the freezing of relatively modest amounts of North American assistance to destabilize the national political system as a whole.[153] However, elsewhere too the old saw that peace carries a lower price-tag than war and may be variably funded without undue risk in *post bellum* conditions was being tested. Whilst there were few signs outside Nicaragua of resumed or escalated hostilities, failure to address the economic consequences of the displacement of hundreds of thousands of people was as threatening in the long term as it was plausible and cheap in the short. It is surely the case that Protestant evangelism has flourished amongst these sectors, the same right-wing groups in the US that subsidized the Contras in the 1980s now propagating a message of self-denial and subordination with rather more modulation, but the claims for the depth and extent of their influence have been made so forcefully as to encourage some caution, particularly in terms of the relation between formal subscription and profound commitment.[154] Neither local governments nor Washington can assume that war-weariness, hunger and deprivation have readily translated into ideological submission.

Elections and the Rule of Law

During the 1980s much of the comment on Central American elections was polarized between those who saw them as 'demonstration polls' designed by the US to throw a veil over essentially dictatorial structures, and those who continuously celebrated them as manifestations of a burgeoning democratic culture. Apart from anything else, these approaches did little to develop the region's notably weak psephological skills with the result that it was very hard to obtain solid evidence either to support such views or to substantiate the plausible hypotheses that even unfair elections produce some competition of consequence and that open polls may keep societies closed. It is, though, noteworthy that the mechanisms and culture of elections themselves became issues of sharp contention during the decade. With the exception of Costa Rica, this focus of controversy may be attributed to three main factors: the much greater use of liberal political procedures to legitimize authoritarian regimes than was the case in South America in the 1960s and 1970s; the holding of polls in the midst of civil wars; and the single-minded, but highly selective, attention paid by Washington to elections in presenting its regional policy.

These distinct but complementary currents lie behind the significant change in Central America's formal constitutions, either through the introduction of completely new political charters – El Salvador (1983); Guatemala (1985); Nicaragua (1987) – or through important reforms – Honduras (in 1981 and 1982 to the constitution of 1965) and Panama (in 1978 and 1983 to the constitution of 1972). Between 1980 and the end of 1993 there were in the region twenty-five separate electoral contests at national level (Appendix 10). Since 1987 every country except Panama has kept to its formal (or in the case of Nicaragua, legally altered) electoral calendar. It is also of some importance that during this period each country witnessed at least one presidential victory by an opposition party, all of these victories being respected – again bar that in Panama in May 1989.[155]

On the other hand, as indicated in Appendix 11, levels of popular abstention were sufficiently high as to cast serious doubt on the locally perceived meaningfulness of this conduct. Whilst there might be a presentable 'contentment thesis' for low voter turn-out in some parts of the world – even the USA, despite notorious difficulties over registration – this is scarcely applicable to Central America, and in Costa Rica, the one consistently functioning liberal democracy, participation rates are complicated by mandatory voting since 1962 (still producing an average abstention rate of 19 per cent).[156] In the case of Guatemala, for example, blank votes topped the poll with 23 per cent of those cast in the constituent assembly elections of 1984 which followed six years of extensive armed conflict and nearly fifteen years of regimes headed by army officers (four elections and two coups). Low popular identification with either the process – as participation – or the outcome – as contestation – of subsequent polls is fully evident in abstention rates that never fell beneath 37 per cent of registered voters and which rose to 70 per cent in the partial municipal elections of May 1993, which were flagrantly manipulated by the ruling Movimiento de Acción Solidaria (MAS).[157] In the case of Guatemala the argument that abstention derives from lack of representation is compelling since no authentically radical organization has been permitted to contest a poll since November 1950, and the incentives for tactical voting for the centre were diminished by the depressing record of the Méndez Montenegro (1966–70) and Cerezo (1986–91) governments. The introduction of a second, run-off round in presidential polls has done little to improve participation. This was also true in El Salvador, where an important current of the left that had engaged in electoral politics in the 1970s under military supervision attempted to contest the elections of 1989 and 1991 under extremely disadvantageous conditions.

Gramsci once famously remarked that elections were only the end of a long process, and the left has traditionally stressed the process, usually at the cost of misjudging the skills and institutions required for elections (which are, of course, as much the start and middle as the end of any process, even if it is in their nature to be celebrated periodically and thus be subject to a particularly chronological reification). In this regard it is worth noting that even parties, such as the Guatemalan Christian Democrats (DCG), that have participated in deeply flawed electoral systems have thereby acquired operational skills and systems lacking in excluded organizations. Age and the attendant familiarity and loyalty have been core assets for established parties, even where failure to win office has precluded the distribution of rewards or threatened a sense of impotence and exhaustion.[158] This pattern is evident elsewhere in Latin America too, but it may be particularly strong in the immediate post-dictatorial period, when popular apprehension places a premium on 'safe' opposition rather than the qualitatively new. Certainly, some such features can be discerned in the initial advantage of the Guatemalan DCG over the neo-conservatives of the UCN; in support for Chamorro, rather than the ultramontane elements of UNO, in Nicaragua; in the resilience of Honduran Liberalism; and in the clear failure of ARENA to monopolize Salvadorean conservatism.

Against this, the promise of change and the opportunities for a belligerent populism have clearly affected the character and outcome of Central American political contests since the late 1980s. Such a process manifestly began on the right of the ideological spectrum – ARENA; Mayor Alemán of Managua; a revived Ríos Montt in Guatemala – but the conditions are little less propitious for the left where it is capable of staging a campaign (everywhere bar Honduras) and participating in the poll (everywhere bar Guatemala and Honduras) however poor the short-term prospects for success might be. Outside of Costa Rica, this experience – both of authentic campaigning and of different resulting governments and balances of official power – was by mid 1993 still very slight in terms of setting patterns of political custom and expectation. No significant new political force had appeared at all after a decade in Honduras. In Nicaragua the historic poll of 1990 was the result of a negative vote that might prove either to be unique or the beginning of an 'exchange pattern' of administrative replacement. (Although it proved impossible to secure this between the Liberals and Conservatives between 1893 and 1936). In El Salvador the artificial contest between the PDC and ARENA during the 1980s had yet to be altered by genuine participation on the part of the left. And in Guatemala neither the left itself nor the traditional institutions of the state were ready to hazard the entry of radicalism into formal competition. One must, therefore, talk of 'pacification' in terms of political transition, rather than the consolidation of liberal democratic institutions and culture, the development of which will depend acutely upon the electoral calendar of the mid 1990s as well as upon deeper shifts in economy and society.[159]

One often overlooked feature in this regard is the growing profile of local and regional electoral contests and politics. Although real controversy over the Central American Parliament (PARLACEN) has not extended beyond Costa Rica, which traditionally fights shy of regional organizations and possibly contagious commitments, accelerated economic integration, international treaties that directly affect popular interests, and the tenuous hold of national identity and ideology suggest potential for an isthmian political forum.[160] Of much more immediate concern to ordinary folk, however, was the redistributive resource and relatively modest demand-performance gap offered by local administration, which also demonstrated occasional signs of balancing – rather than replicating – ideological tendencies on the national stage. Such a tendency in El Salvador during the 1960s and 1970s developed into an especially strong national challenge by reformist forces, and it would not be exotic to imagine contemporary Salvadorean voters supporting the FMLN ticket for local government more extensively – at least in the early stages – than for national office. Certainly, the FMLN itself recognized the importance of local politics and administration in the mid 1980s, its commanders expending much energy in attacking provincial mayors on the grounds that their offices served as counter-insurgency centres and were thus legitimate military targets. Although by 1989 the guerrillas had killed only eleven mayors, nearly half of those elected resigned their posts, and some sixty-four lived and worked away from their homes.

In Guatemala a weaker but not dissimilar effort in the 1970s to forge a reformist challenge out of a foothold in local government was bloodily thwarted, and given the economic and political importance of services – particularly transport – in Central America's largest city, this may still be too dangerous for a power bloc with a keen memory of the riots of the late 1970s and the 1980s. All the same, local politics, especially in the capital cities, can no longer be expected to be a simple administrative echo of national government.

The polls scheduled at all levels for the 1990s will undoubtedly test the tenuous stability and probity of electoral administration, and indeed the institutionalization of the judiciary as a whole. Even in Costa Rica, where the electoral authorities have been genuinely independent since 1949, the office of ombudsman was controversially created in 1993, and some members of the Supreme Court displayed distinctly suspect behaviour. Political manipulation of the courts has been most explicit in Guatemala, Honduras and El Salvador, where there was a clear basis to opposition charges of a lack of division of powers.[161] In the cases of Honduras and Guatemala, control of the judiciary has remained as overtly political in the constitutional period as under the dictatorships, leading to open conflict over spoils (Honduras 1985; Guatemala 1993), extensive decay of the notion of impartiality, and need for wholesale reform. In El Salvador the FMLN succeeded in including in the peace settlement the removal of the government's control of a majority of the appointments to the Supreme Court, a more equitable system to be introduced in 1994. Yet the conduct of many trial judges in a period still dominated by fear and threats remained highly questionable and widely criticized, not least in the USA. According to a report submitted in 1983 to the US secretary of state by US Judge Harold Tyler, 'A handful of inexperienced, undereducated and occasionally corrupt prosecutors represent a society that seems to have lost its will to bring to justice those who commit crimes against it. Intimidation and corruption of prosecutors, judges and juries are widespread.'[162]

This position had not altered a great deal by the end of the 1980s, and prevailed to a similar degree in Honduras and Guatemala. On the other hand, we should note that in El Salvador (Jesuit case) and Honduras (Ricci Mabel Martínez case) a very few military figures have been successfully tried for murder, breaking a tradition of impunity that has either subsisted upon a fearful immobilism or been explicitly sanctioned by amnesty. The regional treatment of war crimes remains undeveloped and is likely to be distended, even if conditions vary significantly from those in South America, where the mechanisms for conducting and terminating judicial review of human rights violations by the armed forces continue to be contested and lie only partially within the realm of official justice. However, both those examples and that of El Salvador clearly indicate that the negotiation of the procedures for settling such matters lies at the very heart of the process of pacification.

The breadth of formal possibilities in this regard is quite impressive although in practice it is unlikely that any Central American model might replicate the experiences of Uruguay (popular plebiscite); Argentina (deadline for indictments, or *punto final*); Chile (proposed hearing of evidence in camera); or Bolivia (escape of dictator in midst of trial). There is, though, a strong tendency to emulate the Southern Cone's emphasis on revelation of the facts ('truth' in the face of disappearance and silence) and a stress on acquiring and expressing knowledge of crimes that very frequently cannot be brought to court. It is possibly the case that this movement – most pronounced in El Salvador, evident in Honduras and likely to develop in Guatemala – has roots in customs engendered by Roman law, most particularly the *denuncia* to an investigating magistrate. However, it plainly also derives from a popular need for public judgement in the likely absence of punishment, through de facto or de jure pardon. Effectively absent from the Esquipulas accords, this issue has failed to come to the fore in Nicaragua, where the conservative opposition was not physically persecuted to any appreciable degree by the Sandinistas, except insofar as the FSLN came under pressure to release Contra and ex-National Guardsmen prisoners. By contrast, the Salvadorean FMLN placed the matter at the centre of their demands during the negotiations of 1990–91, and could hardly have acquiesced in the eventual amnesty introduced by the Cristiani government had there not been an investigation and publication of the major war crimes committed over the previous ten years by the (internationally staffed) Truth Commission (April 1993) and a review of the human rights and professional records of the members of the officer corps by the (Salvadorean) Ad Hoc Commission (September 1992). The appointment of a similar Ad Hoc Commission in Honduras was more surprising and a direct – albeit pre-emptive – initiative on the part of the Callejas government, which rather adroitly shadowed popular sentiment on this matter.

The experience of Guatemala has been both less and more developed in the sense that during the eight years of civilian administration the military easily resisted even discussing any future treatment of the extensive violation of human rights in the 1980s – under Cerezo only one case of the 3,000 reported went to court. And yet in the crisis of 1993 it was precisely the office of ombudsman, virtually bereft of powers other than to receive allegations and evidence, that commanded greatest public respect, and its current occupant, Ramiro de León Carpio, eventually became president of the republic.[163] An apparently minor, 'safety valve' position initially adopted to produce a low-conflict response to human rights pressure had been progressively transformed by internal and external influence into a core catalyst for change. Yet even before this occurred the post was being adopted elsewhere in the region, including Costa Rica, as it became evident to governments that human rights questions were rapidly losing their ideological slant, and any form of injustice administered in the name of the state was liable to provoke complaint.

It is a partial but still telling feature of Central American public life in the early 1990s that governments felt the need to legitimize themselves through such moves, even at the risk of their 'escalation' into mobilization for civil rights, the rule of law and a genuine division of powers. At the same time, long-standing retention of the formal judicial apparatus, fetishization of procedure, and the not unconnected conviction that only new legislation can harm vested interests may combine to offset the threatening or corruption of judges, the intimidation or absence of juries, popular fatalism, and the lack of resources.

The final but crucial element in such a combination is external, in the form of international law as well as the mediation and arbitration provided by foreign and international bodies (UN, OAS, International Court of Justice, etc.), as distinct from the variable political objectives but constantly partisan pressure exercised by the USA. The important role played by the UN after 1990 – predominantly in El Salvador – also, of course, reflects a post-Cold War global tendency. Since there has been a marked narrowing of the terms of peace-making and a corresponding increase in the importance of reciprocal compliance, the UN's particular strengths in observation and documentation are readily applicable.

Yet as the crises of 1993 in both Guatemala and Nicaragua amply demonstrated, where there is either a major imbalance between the forces in contention (URNG and armed forces in Guatemala) or a collapse in trust between the parties in conflict (Recontras and UNO against government and FSLN in Nicaragua) other external agents are required to cajole them into productive exchange. The notion that this can only be done decisively by the US is superficially compelling but not wholly convincing, if only because neither its skills nor its policy over the last fifteen years have been devoted to peace-making except via threat, veto and outright coercion. This, allied with a much – indeed, irresponsibly – diminished interest in Central American affairs in Washington under Clinton, suggests a 'long-stop' role whereby, as in the Nicaraguan kidnap affair, the US signals a general limit to its tolerance but remains content to allow other agents – in this case the region's foreign ministers – to act as principal arbitrators for what are viewed as essentially 'tactical' transgressions. Where such matters are incremental and do not relate to any formal agreement, as in the case of Guatemala, it is very far from clear that there exists in Washington the political interest or will to go beyond intermittent criticism or the individual initiatives of concerned diplomats.

Nicaragua

More than three years after Violeta Chamorro defeated the Sandinistas at the polls, Nicaragua appeared to be on the brink of civil war and seemed to be pacified only in the most tenuous and formal sense. In the first eight months of 1993 over 300 people were killed in armed clashes provoked by outlaw former members of the Contra and EPS, some 2,000 of whom roamed in the north and centre of the country.[164] Moreover, the central political institutions of the post-revolutionary state were sharply disputed: the National Assembly remained boycotted by the bulk of the parties that comprised the victorious UNO alliance of 1990, one of their major demands being the removal of General Humberto Ortega as chief of the EPS, which was much diminished but still very powerful. This was also the central demand of both the ex-Contras who kidnapped thirty-seven people in the northern town of Quilalí in August 1993 and of US Senator Jesse Helms, who in June 1992 attacked the Chamorro administration for its tacit alliance with the FSLN and succeeded in freezing $104 million in US aid for the better part of a year. Helms's invectives against the centrist *concertación* stitched up between the Chamorro team and the Sandinistas acted as a green light to the right-wing extremists in UNO as well as to the remnants of the Contra force, the senator's capacity to cut off finance to Managua having an effect not dissimilar to Colonel North's direct funding of Managua's enemies in the 1980s.

The prospects for any authentic pacification seemed bleak in the extreme when individual US mavericks – even specimens as resolute as these – could exercise such an influence on the affairs of a nominally sovereign country. But the deeper cause for this corrosive and enervating instability was Central America's most profound economic crisis (Appendix 6), which Chamorro's administration could not alleviate even with such US aid as it did receive. This collapse in both production and employment was felt most acutely by ex-combatants, very few of whom had received the land and credit – still less the severance pay – promised in numerous agreements but most particularly in the 'Managua Protocol' of 30 May 1990 between Antonio Lacayo, the new minister of the presidency, and the leading commanders of some 18,000 Contra troops. Three years later the rump of this force was engaged in banditry – as were perhaps 1,000 of the 65,000 EPS troops demobilized over the same period – for which neither international diplomacy nor ideological abuse provided a practical response. At the same time, the acute social tension caused by the withering economic position obliged the FSLN to support popular demands and mobilization against the government, as in the transport strike of September 1993. This too led to deaths and renewed polarization, to all intents and purposes ending the very fragile truce upon which governability had hitherto rested.

Such an image of political decay and a collapse of public order in the midst of the pauperization of the populace is not inaccurate. But neither is it the entire picture, and it may readily be distorted for the purposes of interested homilies about post-revolutionary chaos or subversive accords with Sandinismo. Even at a very high cost, the first three years of the Chamorro government did succeed in demobilizing some 100,000 soldiers, removing the direct military threat to the post-1979 state. Whilst law and order remain extremely fragile in rural Nicaragua, conflict is in no sense comparable to that witnessed during the Contra war of 1981–89, when, according to the EPS, over 20,000 counter-revolutionary troops were killed.[165] Furthermore, the prospects for complete collapse into renewed civil war were markedly lessened for a substantial period by what amounted to a reconstitution of the 1978–79 anti-Somoza alliance between the FSLN (led by the Tercerista Ortega group) and a reformist sector of the bourgeoisie, known now as the 'Las

Palmas' group, headed by Chamorro, and largely staffed by closely related members of a technocratic elite to whom the loud revanchism of the UNO traditionalists was counter-productive and even unseemly.[166] This renewed accord was at no stage enshrined in a formal and comprehensive document, and it remained sharply contested both within the FSLN, which had perforce been opened to internal debate since February 1990, and inside the government, which by September 1993 was ready to alter the leadership of the EPS and even to enter into open confrontation with Sandinismo. Nevertheless, one may clearly discern the importance of an earlier convergence in a number of encounters that suggest the commonly identified 'historical watershed' of the February 1990 elections to be rather less decisive than it initially appeared. Indeed, apart from strong elements of continuity between the deflationary Sandinista economic policy of the late 1980s and that of the more sharply anti-populist Chamorro administration, it is also possible to detect an internal deepening of the Esquipulas process (outlined in Table 2) in which the election marked less a qualitative turning point than a practical consolidation – through a centrist concordat – of agreements previously struck between polarized antagonists. It is easy to over-emphasize this argument as a form of solace against the doleful reality of Nicaragua in the mid 1990s, but it should at least be rehearsed carefully as a counter-weight to the still fiercely ideologized perspectives inherited from the 1980s, sustained by necessary rhetoric, and fortified by memories of loss, heroism and suffering instilled by a decade of civil war.

The differences between the Chamorro/Lacayo group and the right wing of UNO were clear from the very start. On the day he handed office over to Doña Violeta, Daniel Ortega published a newspaper article in Spain in which he declared that UNO possessed

> an extremist faction, led by Vice-President Godoy, which sees our election defeat not as part of a normal transfer of power but as a victory for the counter-revolution. They want heads to fall. There can be no doubt that our position will be tough, intransigent and combative with anybody who wants to cut off our heads. Mrs Chamorro and her team, by contrast, believe that what has occurred is a popular vote within the framework of the Nicaraguan constitution. They approach the transfer of power as a means by which to strengthen democracy and to obtain the complete disarmament of the Contra.[167]

This distinction was by no means shared within the ranks of the FSLN, some of whom saw the matter as a temporary tactical divergence of no real consequence.[168] However, Ortega's position was clearly based on the highly controversial 'Transition Protocol' signed on 27 March 1990 between Lacayo – effectively Chamorro's prime minister – and Generals Humberto Ortega and Joaquín Cuadra (the EPS chief of staff and Lacayo's cousin). Although rather ignored as a result of the furore over the *piñata* and the general aftershock of the election result, this accord provided critical guarantees to both the FSLN, which committed itself to work with Chamorro to 'achieve lasting peace and democracy within a constitutional framework', and the government, which placed on paper its recognition of the 'integrity and professionalism' of the EPS and its guarantee of the 'existing structure and leadership' of the armed forces.[169] Although Chamorro had made it plain that troop numbers would be drastically reduced, it was evident that she had no intention of replacing Sandinista officers with their old Contra foes, thereby removing a major preoccupation of the officer corps. Indeed, four days before the signing of the protocol, Lacayo entered into another agreement with the Contra leadership in Honduras under which the 9,000 troops outside Nicaragua and the 4,000 within it would be demobilized by the time Chamorro took office.[170] This proved impossible, and a further agreement (19 April) stipulated 10 June as the (also insufficient) deadline, but the principal danger – that of a direct armed clash – was clearly being addressed seriously by the new government.

The 'Transition Protocol' infuriated Godoy and the UNO traditionalists who might not have been seeking quite the kind of pogrom intimated by Daniel Ortega but certainly wished to see a wholesale purge of the military. As a result, UNO split immediately after Chamorro assumed office, only two of the sixteen members of her first cabinet being militants of the fourteen mainstream parties of this highly fractious alliance.[171] Nonetheless, with fifty-one deputies against the FSLN's thirty-nine and more than three times the number of provincial mayors, neither effective exclusion from the cabinet nor the progressive decommissioning of the counter-revolutionary forces appeared to be an immediately critical development for UNO. It was between May and July 1990 that the fault-lines became more starkly evident.

As might be anticipated, the catalyst for open political conflict was the fiercely deflationary policy of the Chamorro government and the response of the Sandinista-dominated trade union movement (FNT). The first encounter occurred in mid May, when some 30,000 state employees staged a national strike in demand of a 200 per cent pay rise to compensate for successive devaluations. Offered only 60 per cent, the workers occupied eight of the state's eleven ministries, brought the capital's transport to a halt, and engaged in running battles with the police. Apprehensive about the Sandinistas' promise to 'rule from below', Chamorro and Lacayo backed off, settling at 100 per cent. However, the Contra leadership used this partial retreat as an excuse to put a brake on demobilization, and in July the FNT returned to the fray. This time some 85,000 workers were involved in an eleven-day general strike in support of a $200 per month pay claim. The action rapidly led to street fighting and the cutting of telephone, electricity and water supplies in Managua. Six people were killed and over one hundred injured before the threat of a major incursion by Contra troops and government charges of a planned Sandinista coup produced a settlement.[172] It was at this point that the FSLN leadership stepped back from encouraging popular mobilization and made good its commitment under the protocol of 27 March. In fact, some of the more revisionist members of the party led by Rafael Solís perceived the July mobilization as fundamentally irresponsible, and Humberto Ortega made much of the fact that the EPS had supported the police in restoring order. Godoy, by contrast, viewed Chamorro's settlement as the crossing of the Rubicon: 'She has caved in to the terror of the Sandinista front. She has abandoned all the people who backed her government. This is a process of suicide.'[173]

Between the strikes of May and July the FSLN held an important assembly at El Crucero in which the election defeat was analysed and a process of self-criticism and policy revision begun. This meeting did not unambiguously assist the FSLN's management of the dilemmas presented by opposition in that the predictable criticism of the party's vanguardism, led by Dora Tellez amongst others, implied a more open response to popular sentiment, which was at that time sharply inclined precisely to the anger and combativity that risked wrecking a centrist truce.[174] Equally, however, the clear threat to the revolution's core achievements and a palpable lack of unity within the FSLN enabled the leadership to maintain the initiative, and the party's first congress was postponed from January to July 1991. This sense of embattlement was sustained over the last months of 1990 as Godoy and UNO focused their campaign on the reversal of the agrarian reform and the removal of both Humberto Ortega and Antonio Lacayo from their posts.

The issue of the agrarian reform acted throughout this period as a token for property relations in general. It was, moreover, a matter about which the March 1990 protocol was silent, and over which the government remained uncertain in the face of heavy UNO pressure led by Alfredo César, the former Contra political leader who was now president of the National Assembly. In June 1991 César led a concerted legislative attempt to enforce an almost comprehensive restoration to the original owners of property confiscated under the Revolution. This provoked a not inconvenient Sandinista walkout from the Assembly, depriving it of a quorum on the eve of the party's congress. However, it was not until November 1991 that the issue came to a head after a series of land occupations designed to forestall the threatened restoration of reform properties to their former owners. A number of violent incidents, the destruction of the tomb of FSLN founder Carlos Fonseca Amador, and the renewed prospect of Contra attacks in a year when sixty people had been killed in the countryside prompted Chamorro and Lacayo into accepting a further agreement with the FSLN. Under this pact the government accepted clear restrictions on its privatization programme in return for a Sandinista promise to demobilize party supporters and defuse popular tension.[175] The FNT leadership was distinctly unhappy with this deal – now publicly dubbed *concertación* – which appeared to be deriving limited political reward from extensive rank and file resistance on economic and social matters. Nonetheless, the agreement was effectively enforced, and for the better part of the next year the Las Palmas–FSLN axis remained quite stable. Indeed, in February 1992 Rafael Solís felt able to revive an idea he had floated after the El Crucero assembly – a formal alliance between the Sandinistas and the governing group on a single slate for the 1996 elections.

This proposal, heretical to an important sector of the FSLN rank and file, reflected the emergence of a small group of Sandinistas who sought to combine the pragmatism of the party leadership with the anti-authoritarian tendencies of many militants, who, however, rejected the initiative by the 'Centre Group' as social democratic and capitulationist. Such contradictory currents were permitted by the compromise over both policy and organization reached at the FSLN Congress of July 1991. There almost half the 581 delegates opposed the idea of the National Directorate standing for re-election on a single slate, but this proposal was carried and the party's leadership maintained unchanged (without a single woman) on the understanding that individual candidacies subjected to a secret ballot would be introduced in 1995. In the words of the reformist Comandante Luis Carrión, 'a rupture too brusque with traditions, even when some of these need change, could have a negative effect on the cohesion and unity of the FSLN'.[176] Such a resolution, together with what was recognized to be insufficient response by the 'Ethics Commission' established at El Crucero, introduced a note of marked dissension and disputation, but it did not provoke open division, and proposed limits on debate were successfully resisted at the cost of preserving the principle of democratic centralism. Although the party did predictably little to develop new substantive policies, criticism over vanguardism extended naturally to its statism and collectivism.[177]

Such broad reconsideration of socio-economic strategy did not entail a diminished defence of the agrarian reform in the face of the Godoy–César offensive. In September 1992 César took direct executive control of the National Assembly whilst Sandinista deputies were on the Pacific Coast assisting in the relief effort following a major tidal wave. In response to this virtual coup within the legislature, the FSLN deepened its alliance with the government by boycotting an Assembly that was now operating a form of dual power, aided and abetted by Jesse Helms and the increasingly pugnacious and influential mayor of Managua, Arnoldo Alemán. César's extraordinary ambush was assuredly encouraged by Helms's ability to persuade President Bush to freeze $104 million in aid in the midst of a hard-fought US election campaign. Moreover, the UNO extremists must have felt emboldened by the publication just prior to the tidal wave of Helms's report, in which Republican Party staffer Deborah de Moss opined that 'Nicaragua is a country overwhelmingly controlled by terrorists, thugs and murderers at the highest level'.[178] In addition to alleging nepotism by Chamorro and Lacayo, de Moss focused on the property question – she claimed with characteristic hyperbole that 450 of the owners of expropriated lands had been or become US citizens – and the issue of Sandinista control of the military. Whilst Lacayo repudiated the report as 'full of lies and slander', Chamorro herself sought to defuse the most threatening challenge yet to her government from the right by ordering some 5,000 claims affecting over 16,000 properties to be settled forthwith. These, though, were not to include those of the Somoza family, and neither did the government permit this offensive to derail the 1991 *concertación* agreement that had produced a perceptible modulation in its general privatization programme.

By early 1993 CORNAP, the corporation charged with transferring some 351 public companies to the private sector, had processed 233 firms in what appeared to be a rapid and radical reversal of the Revolution. Moreover, over two years at least 30,000 workers had formally been laid off under this process.[179] However, privatization had not been halted by widespread resistance and neither had it provoked social violence since, following the strike wave of 1991, it had been largely undertaken in consultation with the unions and involved appreciable transfer of ownership to company workforces, which acquired a quarter of privatized firms.[180] In the countryside 113 farms previously belonging to the state sector (APP) were transferred to some 18,000 members of the ATC union whilst 180 properties were restored to prior owners.[181] In October 1992 much-disparaged compensatory bonds were issued to those who failed to lodge a successful claim, and a government promise to review the legal status of property confiscated between February and April 1990 (the *piñata*) failed to dampen the widespread conviction that ownership would not be further revised to a significant degree under this government.[182] Whilst, as elsewhere, the public sector was radically diminished, this process had not descended into mere asset-stripping or an open auction for holders of dollars. Such a measured response may be attributed in no small degree to the strikes and occupations of 1990 and 1991, and had these not forestalled repossession it is highly likely that this would have unleashed conflict far more violent and extensive than that which was eventually provoked by the excluded veterans of both armies in 1992–93.

By the autumn of 1993 a similarly pragmatic solution prevailed with respect to the other major subject of controversy – the military question. Although the 'tit-for-tat' kidnapping crisis of August seemed to have succeeded in forcing Chamorro into announcing the eventual removal of Humberto Ortega as commander of the EPS – and this step was identified by the FSLN as resulting directly from US browbeating – it was by no means certain that such a move would constitute a violation of the March 1990 protocol, since the position of Ortega as an individual was seen as quite distinct from the alteration of any structures of command or organization.[183] Furthermore, the high command itself was primarily concerned to secure legislative approval for its proposed military law – not least because this made proper provision for pensions, absent in the 1980s and inadequately patched over since 1990 by investing the proceeds of sales of equipment.[184] This necessitated the re-incorporation of UNO into the Assembly, control of which had been returned by the Supreme Court to the Centrist–FSLN bloc in January 1993. As a result, it was now boycotted by forty-four deputies from the right – the government had weaned a handful to its cause – and UNO declared itself to be in open opposition.

Humberto Ortega was not alone in supporting harsh repression for his rebel ex-comrades in Estelí in July 1993; tension between cashiered and serving officers was extremely sharp. Nor, with fourteen years in the post and an exceptionally high international profile, could he plausibly claim that his person was subordinate to his professional position. The strongest evidence following the repression in Estelí and the resolution of the kidnapping crisis the next month was that the high command led by Cuadra and Colonel Osvaldo Lacayo would accept the price demanded by Washington and UNO provided that it was neither publicly traded as such nor demonstrably the thin end of the wedge. As by far the most reduced army in the region they had a strong basis for holding such ground and silently withstanding the crowing over Ortega's removal or a change in the name of the EPS.[185]

The position of the FSLN as a political party was quite different insofar as it had to respond to the escalating social pressure caused by the economic crisis and government policies. By September 1993 this meant risking a complete rupture with the regime and pushing Chamorro back into the arms of the UNO ultras, who were now demanding the removal of the 1987 constitution and the establishment of a constituent assembly. For this reason, at the height of the transport strike of September 1993 provoked by the precipitate increase in vehicle taxes, Daniel Ortega went firmly on to the offensive against the government, warning against a renascent *somocismo* and describing the Chamorro cabinet as 'murderous'.[186] At the same time, the renewal of the US freeze on aid now seemed not so much 'more of the same' as a decisive and deliberate punitive act in support of the right-wing offensive. Manifest drift in the Clinton administration's handling of the crisis in Haiti and its severe difficulties over NAFTA seemed, from a Nicaraguan perspective, to presage a field-day for the revanchist North American right over their old foe, further encouraging UNO to increase the stakes. Under such circumstances the Sandinista centrists were hard pressed to make the case for *concertación*, although UNO's targeting of Lacayo kept the option of a 1996 electoral pact within the realm of the possible. By contrast, the polarization and violence of the September transport strike recalled that of July 1990, similarly pushing at least some of the FSLN leaders down the path of confrontation.

By October 1993 the forces militating for a return to violent conflict and the dissolution of a manageable civil society were formidable. Vandalism and extremist aggression were fomented by both the appalling state of the economy and policy on the part of the radical right. On the other hand, popular exhaustion with violence and military affairs, the clear interest of the rest of the region in a lasting political settlement, and the inability of the North American campaign for a full counter-revolutionary solution to gain White House support represented brakes on polarization.

El Salvador

As has already been highlighted, the Salvadorean peace settlement differs from that in Nicaragua in that, rather than flowing from an international treaty, it was at root a domestic agreement, albeit strongly brokered and invigilated by the UN. Other obvious differences rest in the fact that in El Salvador the government was supported by Washington and the left was in opposition. As a result, although the general weight of US influence was no less – in some respects greater – than in Nicaragua, this took the quite distinctive form of qualified or withdrawn patronage as well as giving a fundamentally rhetorical and partisan defence of liberal democracy greater authenticity. The visit made to San Salvador by Vice-President Bush in 1983 was essentially to secure diplomatically defensible conduct by the government and its army; that undertaken by Vice-President Quayle in February 1989 required much more of the Salvadorean state, even before the collapse of Communism and the near-decisive offensive launched by the FMLN in November of that year.

Rather like the Nicaraguan election of 1990, the undoubted importance of the rebel offensive both as a synthetic expression of developing trends and as an intrinsic crisis has resulted in it frequently being overemphasized by commentators. However, because the Salvadorean civil war was far more evenly balanced than that in Nicaragua, specific operations and their logistics were of correspondingly greater consequence. Equally, whilst the timing of the offensive in the midst of the international collapse of Communism was not directly prompted by events in eastern Europe, neither was it entirely coincidental with external developments. It is a quite accurate reflection of the nature of the Salvadorean civil war that the marked autonomy from foreign influence of the FMLN as well as the changes in Washington meant that the US was not provoked by the offensive into committing troops to forestall the collapse of its client regime. This would, in any case, have been made logistically impossible by the impending invasion of Panama – a fact that should remind us of the intensive activity and sense of crisis that prevailed in and around Central America at the end of Bush's first year in office. In fact, it was at the start of 1989, precisely on the day after the president's inauguration, that the FMLN staged an entirely unexpected initiative – rather as it had done in 1981 just prior to Reagan's inauguration. This time, however, the rebel action was boldly political in character, and by offering to participate in the coming elections if these were postponed by six months (from March to September) and made subject to relatively innocuous guarantees, it appeared to represent a complete volte face, not least because the FMLN had expended much diplomatic and political energy in attacking the elections held since 1982.[187]

In practice, the FMLN initiative was rather less adventurous, and not only because neither the extreme right-wing ARENA nor Washington was expected to respond favourably. (In the event, both they and the PDC treated the rebel proposal remarkably seriously through most of the election campaign for the simple reason that popular desire for an end to the war was so central to the result.) Just as important as this preparedness to float daring proposals was the FMLN's continuing political development, which had gone through a number of broad phases since 1979.[188] The most public of these was the replacing in 1983 of the radical socio-economic programme designed in 1980 for a regime based on a revolutionary seizure of state power. The 1983 platform provided in much more flexible form for a 'government of broad participation' (*gobierno de amplia participación*; GAP), which would include representatives of all major political forces and maintain elements of the existing state army, always provided these had not participated in the violation of human rights. At the core of the 1983 GAP proposal was the integration of the FMLN's forces into any post-settlement military apparatus. This remained a prominent feature of the January 1989 offer and would, indeed, be one of the main rebel demands until September 1991. The insistence upon expulsion and punishment of those responsible for war crimes was likewise constant and became a central element of the peace agreement that was finally signed. Of course, neither of these issues is inherently radical from an ideological viewpoint, but both were of critical importance in the context of a civil war, and by maintaining them until the very last moment the FMLN was responding to a core constituency of fighters and supporters for whom guarantees of security and expression of justice were just as vital as radical economic policies.

Although the 1989 offer represented a significant shift away from the GAP proposals, it did so largely by surrendering the idea of a prolonged provisional government rather than marking a shift of position over electoral competition per se. In fact, even the left's critique of the US-backed official electoral contests between the PDC and ARENA was unravelling as its non-combatant, reformist allies mutated from the Frente Democrático Revolucionario (FDR) into the Convergencia Democrática (CD) and began with extreme caution to test the possibility of involvement in legal politics from late 1987. In the event this did not entail entering the 1988 local and legislative elections, but it clearly signalled the opening of a new political front as well as the prospect of CD participation in the 1989 poll.

The predictable challenge from this quarter was complemented by the accumulating influence of the FMLN's military strategy on its political outlook. Here the key shift came slightly after the GAP proposal, in 1984–85, when it became obvious that the escalation of the guerrilla war into one of substantial military formations was not just problematic but decidedly dangerous. The central feature in this was the difficulty in protecting large numbers of unarmed civilian supporters who lived in 'liberated zones', openly expressed sympathy for the rebels, and were exceptionally vulnerable targets for any counter-attack by the notoriously brutal state army. In essence, by developing from the tactics of clandestine and highly mobile small groups into those that required the holding of territory, the FMLN was sacrificing its popular supporters since it remain incapable of continuously defending territory when attacked in strength. As a result, the guerrillas reduced the number of their troops, shifted their targets, and discouraged supporters from open acts of sympathy, instead urging them to engage in a *doble cara* (two-faced) existence whereby they were free to display support for the legal parties and participate in the comings and goings of official civil society. This inevitably instilled a less manichaean attitude and a greater sensitivity to tactical exigencies and requirements of ordinary folk. In very much the same mould, the FMLN had come to recognize the high social cost of its sabotage campaigns against public transport – which penalized the poor far more sharply than they did the rebels' 'natural' class enemy – even though these were exceptionally efficient from a military and propaganda perspective.[189]

These factors produced a particularly confusing situation. On the one hand, some US advisers confidently opined that 'these guys' units are getting smaller. What more evidence do you want [of rebel decline]?' On the other, the head of military intelligence confessed that he was unable to assess the FMLN's capacity for staging strategic operations.[190] In fact, the guerrilla command considered its January 1989 offer to be opening a 'strategic counter-offensive', in which military operations would be necessary in order to force the regime to negotiate. This assumption appeared to be fully vindicated when Cristiani won the election so emphatically, the FMLN, still publicly at loggerheads with its semi-allies in the CD, failing either to halt the poll or to provide for subsequent initiatives. Moreover, whilst Cristiani's offer at his inauguration (June 1989) to enter into talks without any prior FMLN surrender – the constant demand made by PDC President Duarte – seemed to open the possibility of a straight right–left negotiation without any complicating centrist mediation, the lack of official interest in formal contacts and then the death-squad bombing of the FENASTRAS union office at the end of October convinced the guerrilla leadership that Cristiani had no real intention of talking and was merely adopting a different ruse to Duarte. Consequently, long-standing rebel plans for a major offensive were set in motion, leading to the November assault on San Salvador and several provincial capitals.[191]

The surprise caused in Washington and San Salvador by the FMLN's capacity to sustain this large-scale operation and retreat in good order after ten days' intensive fighting was matched by the widespread repudiation of the military's preparedness to cause civilian casualties in its counter-attacks. As in the past, this disposition became tragically enshrined in the murder of unarmed members of a religious body – in this case the six Jesuit priests and their housekeeper and her daughter executed on the night of 15 November – who were considered by many in the armed forces to be closet rebels and legitimate targets. To a very appreciable extent, the cold-blooded assassination dominated the international perception of the November fighting, making this seem quite similar to the assaults being made on the tyrannies of eastern Europe, where clerics were also being persecuted, albeit by Communists and rarely at the cost of their lives. The damage caused by this made any scare-mongering about an imminent radical takeover quite unproductive on the international plane, and the regime's immediate response in criminalizing the expression of any political opinion other than that of its supporters signalled the price of rejecting talks. At the same time, whilst FMLN fighters in the thick of battle were understandably telling the world's press that they were fighting for 'revolution or death', the rebel leadership maintained a quite consistent attachment to the policy of negotiations, employing the term 'insurrection' far more flexibly than some allowed for.[192]

The position of the right and the state was equally conducive to pacification. The November offensive may have failed to secure a revolutionary seizure of power, but it unambiguously signalled a rebel capacity to continue with a campaign of sabotage that had sorely damaged the economy and cut deep into profits. Moreover, it highlighted the futility of any effort to impose a 'Djakarta solution' – the killing of tens of thousands which was touted by some as an alternative to selective death-squad executions.[193] The fact was, of course, that tens of thousands had already been killed, and whilst talk of massacres might still possess some cathartic property for those on the extreme right, such activity patently lacked deterrent effect at a strategic level. The prospect of a profitable peace began to compete with that of an extirpation of Communists. There was certainly no public entrepreneurial pressure group for negotiations, but Central America's most aggressive mercantilists already had a large target in five years of Christian Democratic interventionism, which in many respects drew fire from the FMLN's putative collectivism. ARENA had long dubbed the PDC cryptocommunist, but now that the radical right finally held both executive and legislative power it needed to translate long-rehearsed free-trade rhetoric into tangible recovery. Without a solution to the war it stood in some danger of simply altering the proprietorial status of rebel targets.

The position within the military was noticeably more rigid. The November offensive starkly revealed the inefficiencies of both the high command and its tactical operations. This was doubly important because in June 1988 what amounted to a coup had taken place within the armed forces with the major commands being occupied by members of the large 1966 graduating class of the military academy. This group was known as the *tandona* because of its fierce attachment to the culture and practices of the *tanda* (cohort) system excoriated by an extremely critical report on the Salvadorean military written by four US colonels in 1988:

> Once each class or *tanda* is commissioned from the Salvadorean military academy, it moves upwards through the ranks together, the group advancing at intervals regardless of any evidence of individual competence or lack thereof. Whatever an officer's personal failings – stupidity, cowardice in battle or moral profligacy – his career is secure through the rank of colonel, after which he may depart, with his *tanda*, into honourable retirement.[194]

In November 1988 the *tandona* took complete control of the military command structure with the appointment as defence minister of General René Emilio Ponce, who had been denied a US visa for several years because of his involvement in human rights abuses.[195] Although the *tandona* leaders espoused a more 'aggressive' prosecution of the war and possessed in ARENA a much more tractable political administration, the US Congressional Research Service had come to the same conclusion as the four colonels: 'the war is stuck. Unhappily, the United States finds itself stuck with the war.'[196] One central and clearly identifiable reason for this incapacity was the corruption within the office corps, encouraged by the large amount of US aid. Amongst the most common forms this took was pay fraud, whereby a sizeable proportion of the 20,000 pay slots budgeted for soldiers each year were filled by phantom conscripts whose wages passed into the hands of local commanders. The fact that the pay of NCOs, key to the army's tactical capacity, was twice that of recruits meant that 'ghosting' these troops was far more profitable but also more detrimental to the war effort.[197] The absence of a central roster and the clannish loyalties of the *tanda* system meant that general knowledge of such rip-offs and their cost was matched by total silence over individual instances and the absence of prosecutions or enforced retirement. Indeed, some US observers were convinced that the Salvadorean officer corps had become so locked into these lucrative scams that they did not wish to win the war and thus lose their North American source of income.[198]

By November 1989 it was apparent that the army could not win the war even if it wished to do so. Overall, it had performed badly enough during the offensive to have lost prestige in its bargaining with the ARENA government, and yet its support was essential to Cristiani's own bargaining with both Washington and the FMLN. More important still, the question of the future role and organization of the military was at the top of a rebel agenda now shorn of all major socio-economic demands. This, in fact, proved to be the most intractable item in the prolonged series of talks listed in Table 4. It was only in September 1991, nearly two years after the offensive, that the FMLN gave way on its requirement to form part of a new military apparatus. As a result of this concession the guerrillas, by progressively demobilizing, would rapidly lose their military capacity to invigilate the peace agreement or provide themselves with guarantees of physical security. Its necessary corollary was not only a remarkably high profile given to the UN verification of the agreements but also government acceptance of extensive investigation of past human rights violations. Both these components were plainly going to damage the military institution as a whole and threatened grave punishment for some of its most senior members whose conduct over the past decade had been based on the confident expectation of impunity. Nonetheless, the army was unable to resist such accords, which were reached in April 1991, at a break-through meeting in Mexico City. By that stage US readiness to cut military assistance had been demonstrated (October 1990) and ARENA had suffered serious setbacks in the legislative and municipal elections (March 1991). Full veto power – long an attribute of a military institution cajoled by the US into accepting civilian government in the early 1980s – had been lost, opening a period of survivalist scape-goating, the pursuit of amnesties, and the revival of a pungent, anti-*gringo* chauvinism that would fuel the public and political careers of the most belligerent officers (Colonel Ochoa, General Bustillo, General Ponce).

The final Salvadorean peace accord effectively amalgamated all the agreements reached over the previous two years. As a consequence, its terms were extensive and complicated.[199] One of its most important features lay in the carefully designed demobilization timetable outlined in Table 5. Complementary to this process, which would totally disarm the FMLN and reduce the army's establishment to around 30,000, was the disbanding of the three state security forces (Guardia Nacional; Policía Nacional; Policía de Hacienda) and the establishment of a new

Table 4 The Origins of the Salvadorean Peace Accord, 1989–92

23 Jan. 1989	El Salvador	FMLN offers to contest and respect elections if these delayed for six months with military confined to barracks.
21 March 1989	El Salvador	Cristiani offers talks; in response FMLN proposes new poll, withdrawal of US military aid, radical reduction of military and trial of those responsible for repression.
1 June 1989	El Salvador	At his inauguration Cristiani offers talks without prior FMLN surrender.
4 April 1990	Geneva	Joint declaration of desire to end war, promote democracy and guarantee human rights; commitment to secret negotiations under mediation of UN Secretary General or his representative.
21 May 1990	Caracas	Three-phase agenda established: political accords sufficient for a ceasefire; integration of FMLN into legal sphere; consolidation of peace. UN to verify all accords. Military represented for first time.
26 July 1990	San José	Substantive agreement on human rights and establishment of ONUSAL, first UN verification body to oversee human rights at end of a civil war.
27 April 1991	Mexico City	Major accord to amend 1983 Constitution, including alteration of role of military, dissolution of military intelligence directorate and three paramilitary bodies, to be replaced by civilian police; new non-partisan electoral tribunal and more broadly elected Supreme Court; Truth Commission to be set up to assess violation of human rights by both sides.
26 July 1991	El Salvador	ONUSAL starts human rights monitoring under broad powers that preclude need for referral to New York.
11 Sept. 1991	El Salvador	New National Assembly ratifies constitutional reform required by Mexico accord of April.
25 Sept. 1991	New York	Rejection of phased ceasefire; FMLN agrees in secret annexe to drop all demands for inclusion of its troops in military in exchange for participation in new police force (PNC); establishment of National Commission for Consolidation of Peace (COPAZ), comprised of parties, with powers to implement accords.
23 Oct. 1991	Washington	US Congress withholds half of military aid pending improvement in human rights and advances in peace process.
31 Dec. 1991	New York	Six-paragraph act ('New York II') ending the civil war is signed; calendar for implementation discussed until 14 Jan.
16 Jan. 1992	Mexico City	Formal signing at Chapultepec Castle of accord consolidating all agreements since April 1991 in presence of new UN Secretary General Boutros Boutros-Ghali and various heads of state.

Table 5 El Salvador Peace Treaty: Formal Timetable for 1992

Jan.	16	Signing of formal accords.
	24	Legal incorporation of COPAZ.
	25	Military to provide ONUSAL with complete arms and troops inventory.
Feb.	1	'D-Day': formal ceasefire starts; end of forced conscription; tabling of legislation to guarantee security of FMLN, COPAZ and other commissions; start of transfer of farms over 245 hectares.
	7	FMLN to start demobilization.
	16	Designation of Supreme Electoral Court.
	18	Deadline for FMLN inventory of land holdings in regions under its control.
Mar.	2	Dissolution of Guardia Nacional and Policía de Hacienda; creation of state intelligence department to replace DNI (to be dissolved by 15 June); designation of human rights ombudsman.
	31	Start of submission of land requests by veterans of both armies.
May	1	Start of demobilization and re-incorporation into civilian life of FMLN troops, to proceed at a monthly rate of at least 20 per cent of fighters.
	16	Installation of Ad Hoc Commission to review records of military officers and recommend removal of human rights violators.
	31	Deadline for reform of electoral system.
June	30	Deadline for dissolution of all paramilitary defence units.
July	14	Legalization of ownership of lands in zones of conflict.
	17	Start of demobilization of army's five elite battalions.
Oct.	13	Start of purge from armed forces of human rights violators.
	31	End of FMLN demobilization.
Dec.	7	End of army's elite battalion demobilization.

national civilian police (PCN) completely separate from the army. The majority of the recruits for this force would not have participated in the civil war, but of those who had equal numbers were to be from the old Policía Nacional and the FMLN.

The peace settlement also made important changes to state institutions in its provisions for the Supreme Court, which, as we have seen, had become heavily politicized and exercised rigid control over lower courts. In future a two-thirds majority of the legislature would be needed for the election of Supreme Court judges (instead of a simple majority), and length of service was increased to nine years, further distancing the court from the political cycle. All political parties would now participate in the preparation of the electoral register, and the Supreme Electoral Tribunal would also be elected by a two-thirds majority of the National Assembly.[200]

The settlement's treatment of the massive violation of human rights since 1980 was two-fold in nature. Taking its lead from the Rettig Commission in Chile, a Truth Commission was set up to provide a selective – but still extensive – review of the worst abuses by all parties, and to make recommendations to prevent any repetition. However, the commission, which was composed of three eminent non-Salvadoreans, possessed only limited powers of recommendation with regard to the punishment of identified individuals.[201] This aspect came more directly under the purview of a second body, the Ad Hoc Commission, which was to review the personal records of military personnel. Unlike the report of the Truth Commission, the findings of this body, composed of Salvadoreans, were not to be published and would be passed, via the UN, directly to the president for action.[202]

The accord called for the complete implementation of the agrarian reform programme begun in 1980, and the government agreed to recognize current tenure of land in conflict zones as well as favouring ex-combatants in the distribution of land under the National Reconstruction Plan (PNR) to be assisted by the UN. Longer-term socio-economic matters would be considered and debated in a new Forum for Economic and Social Consensus constituted by representatives of government, business and labour in equal numbers.

The main organization charged with overseeing the implementation of these agreements was the Commission for the Consolidation of Peace (COPAZ), comprising two representatives from the government, two from the FMLN, and one each from the parties or fronts with seats in the Assembly. However, COPAZ soon proved to be an inefficient and fractious forum, and the main impetus for implementation and verification came from ONUSAL, set up in 1990 with some 150 members from twenty-nine of the UN's member-states. Indeed, had ONUSAL not possessed its unusually strong remit and rapidly established a firm reputation with both sides, even the relatively modest progress over the first eighteen months following the agreement would not have been possible.

The first major difficulty was in mutual compliance over demobilization, both sides exploiting ambiguities in the formal treaty to test each other's nerve, but in November 1992 the FMLN won public UN support for its argument that it was not obliged to keep to a timetable if the government failed to respect complementary agreements. Thus, in April Cristiani attempted to circumvent the disbandment of the paramilitary forces by means of simply changing their names (rather as had Pinochet in Chile), and for a week at the end of October the demobilization was halted in a tense stand-off requiring strenuous UN arbitration before an extended timetable (to 15 December) was accepted. The question of demobilization was revived in no less critical a fashion with the revelation of clandestine FMLN arms guerrilla by the explosion of 23 May 1993 in Managua.[203] The scale of stocks subsequently admitted, the embarrassment caused to UN Secretary General Boutros-Ghali (who had publicly accepted the rebels' assurances of complete disarmament), and the damage done to the FMLN's reputation by its transgression all played into the hands of the San Salvador government and conservative forces. On the other hand, Cristiani conspicuously failed to fulfil his obligation to act on the Ad Hoc Commission report by the end of November 1992. According to most reliable sources, he was obliged to remove or reassign some hundred officers, including General Ponce and many of his senior colleagues, identified with specific violations of human rights.[204] This move was taken only in March 1993, and then heavily qualified by the issuing of an amnesty for all those accused of crimes (except kidnapping and drug-smuggling) during the war. The amnesty announcement was made the day before the publication of the Truth Commission report, and it appeared to have the acquiescence of the guerrilla leadership, although human rights organizations and the relatives of the victims expressed great anguish, the National Human Rights Commission petitioned the Supreme Court to rule the amnesty unconstitutional, and even the US State Department attacked it as a guarantee of impunity.[205] In some respects the amnesty was made both inevitable and more provocative by the publication of the Truth Commission report (15 March 1993). This long and detailed document addressed cases involving the killing of some 23,000 people, including the 1989 assassination of the Jesuits and the massacres of the early 1980s, the awful details of which were also being revealed at the time by teams of forensic anthropologists. The commission attributed 85 per cent of violations to the state forces and only 5 per cent to the FMLN. In the same vein, it recommended the immediate dismissal of some forty senior officers, who would be banned from holding public office for ten years, as would three FMLN *comandantes* (Joaquín Villalobos; Ana Guadalupe Martínez; and Jorge Meléndez of the ERP) of the fifteen identified as having committed abuses.[206] Whilst the FMLN accepted all the commission's recommendations, the Supreme Court joined the high command in attacking it, and attempted (without success) to resist its provisions on the grounds that it had been set up under agreements between the FMLN and the executive branch – not the judiciary – and so its findings were not binding.[207]

A similarly clouded experience resulted from the peace agreement's plans for the new police force, which was woefully under-funded and very slowly assembled, and the distribution of land, which had been slow from the start and by May 1993 amounted to only 9,700 grants of the 47,500 agreed in December 1992.[208] The erratic, under-funded and much-disputed process of land titling provoked frequent occupations of rural properties which the government and landlords depicted as guerrilla attempts to destabilize the accords at the same time as Cristiani celebrated the allocation of plots as a major triumph for private property and popular capitalism.[209] However, none of these insufficiencies, manipulations and interested interpretations amounted to a decisive challenge to the peace settlement, which by mid 1993 appeared much more secure than that in Nicaragua. One factor in this was undoubtedly the proximity of the presidential election of March 1994, focusing the political attention of all parties. The differences that predictably opened up within both the right- and the left-wing alliances as a result of the cessation of hostilities did provoke a modicum of violence as old scores were settled.[210] Nevertheless, the more important consequence of this was the extension of competition and re-assessment of alliances that had been frozen for almost a dozen years and not subjected to authentic electoral challenge since 1972.[211]

Guatemala

The pattern of Guatemalan politics over the six years since the signing of the Esquipulas treaty was distinct from those in Nicaragua and El Salvador insofar as there was no formal peace agreement between the guerrillas and the government – not even a partial ceasefire. Moreover, the negotiations between the URNG and the state were not in themselves a central feature of public life since the guerrilla challenge in Guatemala was far weaker than in El Salvador and lacked the powerful external allies possessed by the Nicaraguan Contra. Expectations that the administration established by Human Rights Ombudsman Ramiro de León Carpio in the wake of the crisis of May–June 1993 might reach a rapid truce with the URNG were misplaced. In the first place the undeniably important implosion of the system of civilian government set up in 1986 had only slight short-term repercussions on the military, and the officer corps was far more strongly placed than its Salvadorean counterpart in 1989. Secondly, the perceptible increase in guerrilla activity in 1990 that encouraged some abroad to imagine a scenario akin to that in El Salvador in November 1989 was, in fact, the prelude to a decisive campaign by the army, not the URNG, which had been reduced to a marginal force before the civic crisis of mid 1993. As a result, a sizeable portion of the military establishment considered the notion of negotiation thoroughly ignoble. On the other side, the URNG was patently too weak to countenance a rapid series of concessions of the type accepted by the FMLN late in 1991.

Reactions abroad to the collapse of President Serrano's May 1993 *autogolpe* ('self-coup') understandably registered hope that the initial momentum of the crisis might carry through into the new government's actions. When that failed to occur there was a noticeable over-reaction by commentators who now predicted sell-outs, oligarchic ambushes and a renewal of the culture of control set up in 1954. This view may well prove to be justified, but after nearly forty years of a singularly autocratic regime, Guatemalan civil society manifestly operated with enormous caution, especially since the advocates of revolution had been strategically subjugated. Political and cultural re-adjustment was always likely to be more prolonged and hesitant than in El Salvador and Nicaragua, and not only because of the weight of an indigenous population that had borne the brunt of the massacres of 1978–83. This profound lack of trust, and the suspicion prompted by even the most modest overtures or opportunities is most evident on the left in the reaction of the popular movement to the collapse of Serrano's auto-cratic endeavour. For a number of days the leadership of the country's human rights and trade union organizations proved unable to move beyond formulaic denunciation of the feverish attempts by the political and military elite to extricate itself from the crisis. Much of the polemic simply identified these efforts as a military counter-coup and failed to pose plausible alternatives that might have positively exploited the tangible distress of traditional antagonists. De León Carpio was eventually able to take office, but the lack of initiative from his supporters bore all the hallmarks of two generations of repression and two episodes (1966–70; 1986–93) of broken promises of constitutional propriety. Popular political skills were as slight as the resilience of the masses was deep.

Such reticence was reciprocated by the right, which was able to use continued guerrilla actions as an excuse for avoiding genuine concessions. Guatemala, it should be recalled, had been a very early and immediate victim of the Cold War. The counter-revolution of 1954 was no medium-distance influence but a major watershed in the nation's life, armouring an elite culture of anti-Communism that pre-dated the revolution in Cuba – let alone that in Nicaragua – and even displayed some of the traumas caused by Mexican radicalism in the 1930s. In its own view the right also had historic experience of 'pseudo-democracy' under the reformist regimes of Arévalo and Arbenz

(1944–54). Moreover, its nationalist reflexes had been fully exercised from the mid 1970s by Carter's criticism and withdrawal of aid because of human rights abuses, and then by the US Congress's refusal to restore to Guatemala the support so energetically championed by Reagan. Far more accustomed to pariah status than were the Salvadorean and Nicaraguan ruling classes, and with far more to show for its scorched-earth policies, the Guatemalan elite was exceptionally difficult to budge, if not absolutely intractable.

One element of flexibility was given, as we have seen, by economic change in the form of *maquila*, a shift away from traditional exports and the rigid plantation cultures that upheld them, and the challenge presented by NAFTA. Another was the price paid for possessing constitutional government since the mid 1980s: the promotion of unevenly skilled politicians many of whom lacked publicly acceptable ethics or a capacity to modulate their greed according to circumstances. A third feature was the experience of unexpected, spontaneous rioting in the capital (1978; 1985; 1990) caused by economic policy, especially with regard to bus fares and electricity prices. In both cases this reflected a long-standing resistance to increased funding through taxation, but now maladministration and cavalier pillaging threatened to transform a serious recurrent problem into an irreversible crisis. The habitual response to this – unhampered repression – was precisely what the artifice of constitutionalism was designed to avoid. The attendant degeneration of the legitimacy of the 'new democrats' – principally the Christian Democrats and Serrano's MAS but also elements of the decrepit Partido Revolucionario (PR) and the neo-conservative Unión Centrista Nacional (UCN) – plainly required some reconsideration of the historic options open to the power bloc.

The failure of the URNG on the battlefield makes it unlikely that any eventual Guatemalan peace settlement will go much further than the rebels' demobilization, re-incorporation into the legal sphere (the legitimacy of which they would recognize in exchange for an amnesty) and, if conditions were propitious, some judicial consideration of the violation of human rights since the late 1970s. Any concessions beyond this on the government side were more likely to stem from its own initiative or accumulating pressure from the popular movement than from rebel bargaining.[212] At the root of such a balance of forces was the success of the military's scorched-earth policies of the late 1970s and – when its blanket terror proved counter-productive in 1981–82 – the introduction of a more considered system of free-fire zones, strategic hamlets, civic action and civilian conscription (the Patrullas de Autodefensa Civil – PACs). In the words of General Héctor Gramajo, army commander and defence minister for much of the 1980s, 'Before, the strategy was to kill 100 per cent ... But you don't need to kill everybody to complete the job ... There are more sophisticated means ... We instituted civil affairs [in 1982], which provides development for 70 per cent of the population while we kill 30 per cent.'[213] The candour of Gramajo's statement shocks, but the abundant documentation that has been accumulated over the last dozen years strongly suggests that, at least with respect to the central highlands of the country, he was not boasting without cause.[214] Although the figures are necessarily provisional and partial, we may talk without fear of exaggeration of 30,000 people killed during the 1980s, 150,000 displaced within the country, and 50,000 taking refuge in Mexico. The most sober estimates refer to 30,000 widows, 38,000 children completely orphaned, and 90,000 losing one parent.[215] In addition, one must take into account the traumatic impact on some 50,000 people of resettlement in one of the two dozen closely vigilated model villages, and the frequently coerced conscription of at least 725,000 men into the PACs – subject as much to the whims of local *caciques* and military commanders as to URNG attacks.[216]

Such numbers make plausible references to the militarization of Guatemalan society, particularly in the countryside, where most of the fighting has taken place and where most of its victims live or lived. The army has undoubtedly succeeded in altering the outlook and attitudes of many rural Guatemalans, whether indigenous or *ladino*; and over the last ten years the scale of its organizational activity as well as more directly military operations raise doubts as to the accuracy and usefulness of depicting it as simply murderous and repugnant to local people.[217] Its success has taken time – civic action programmes rarely yield results rapidly – but it is manifestly based on more than coercive control. For this reason all the substantive proposals of the URNG, which has no more than 2,000 guerrilla fighters, focus on the dismantling of the institutions of the counter-insurgency strategy – far more extensive and autonomous than those in El Salvador – as well as investigation of human rights violations.

The first step in the fragile process of negotiation came in September 1987, under the Esquipulas agreement, which provided only a loose framework since neither the URNG nor the military received significant external support and were therefore not very susceptible to the treaty's provision in that respect. The establishment of the National Reconciliation Commission (CNR) under the presidency of the Bishop of Esquipulas, Monsignor Rodolfo Quezada, was obligatory under the terms of the treaty but also a step willingly taken by the Christian

Democratic administration of Vinicio Cerezo, who had come to office eighteen months earlier. Although Cerezo was disarmingly direct about his very modest ambitions for this first civilian administration, and he could not countenance presenting the high command with a major challenge, the president needed at least to be seen to be taking a different approach to that of his military predecessors.[218] In the event, Cerezo was not faced with a taxing dilemma because when, in October 1987, the URNG met the CNR in Madrid, the rebel proposals were palpably unacceptable to the army, which responded by imposing an effective veto on further contacts until March 1991. Most of the guerrillas' demands were radical only in the context of the Guatemalan civil war, which by that stage had mutated into a very one-sided conflict. The most obvious demands were for the abolition of the PACs, model villages and 'development poles' run by the army; unrestricted movement within the country; full respect for human rights and freedom of free speech and association; application of the Geneva Convention; and a formal dialogue between the major social and economic forces in the country. However, the proposals that most directly antagonized the officer corps were for the institution of a 'Truth Commission' and the establishment of demilitarized zones. Although Quezada proved a highly energetic president of the CNR and, rather like Cardenal Obando y Bravo in Nicaragua, possessed sufficient understanding of the rebels to retain their trust, neither military nor political forces favoured his cause.

What may be seen as a prolonged second attempt to settle the Guatemalan war is sketched in Table 6. This process began with the Oslo meeting between the URNG and the CNR in March 1990, nearly two years after their last public encounter. There was little sign of a shift in the high command's position at this time, but external factors had now changed considerably. Less than a month earlier the Sandinistas had been voted out of office, and Washington, influenced by both that development and the earlier FMLN offensive in El Salvador, was now seeking in earnest to secure a solution in Guatemala, which not only formed part of the conflictive Central American arena but also bordered on Mexico, and thus the projected North American Free Trade Area.

The principal problem for the US was the limited purchase it had on a military establishment to which it issued virtually no cash, which it had not trained in significant numbers for fifteen years, and which now possessed a markedly autonomous disposition. Clearly, Washington could not hope to secure a resolution either at a comparable speed to those in Nicaragua and El Salvador or with corresponding expectations of its own interests being met. In December 1989, in the immediate

Table 6 The Guatemalan Peace Process, 1987–92

9 Sept. 1987	Guatemala	Establishment of National Reconciliation Commission (CNR) under presidency of Bishop of Esquipulas, Rodolfo Quezada.
9 Oct. 1987	Madrid	First public contact between rebel and state representatives for twenty-seven years ends without accord.
23 Aug. 1988	San José	First URNG–CNR talks.
30 March 1990	Oslo	Second URNG–CNR meeting under auspices of World Lutheran Federation; general accord to resolve conflict by political means and set up mechanisms for resolving basic problems of Guatemalan society; Quezada to act as 'Conciliator' and UN Secretary General invited to observe.
1 June 1990	Madrid	'Agreement of Escorial' signed by URNG and main political parties envisages legalization of rebels, who pledge not to disrupt November poll.
1 Sept. 1990	Ottawa	URNG talks with business confederation CACIF; no accord or joint communiqué on rebel economic demands for increased production, wage rises, land reform; more jobs and agricultural diversification.
26 Sept. 1990	Quito	URNG–Church agreement to support constitutional reform, respect human rights and condemn economic and social marginalization.
27 Oct. 1990	Metepec/ Atlixco, Mexico	URNG meets representatives of twenty-three organizations and academics. Declarations support direct talks with government; establishment of constituent assembly to remove repressive state apparatus; role of CNR as principal mediating body.
26 April 1991	Mexico DF	First official URNG–government talks agree eleven-point agenda for negotiations, including socio-economic issues.
22 June 1991	Querétaro, Mexico	Second round of talks; general agreement on first agenda item – democratic principles for state and civil society.
24 Sept. 1991	Mexico DF	Failure to agree on human rights.
21 Oct. 1991	Mexico DF	Failure to agree on human rights.
25 Jan. 1992	Mexico DF	Failure to agree on human rights.
15 May 1992	Guatemala	New URNG proposals omit points 8 – 11 of April 1991 agenda (on mechanisms for demobilization and legalization) and focus on refugee resettlement, reform of constitution, indigenous rights and economic change as prerequisites for talks.
7 Aug. 1992	Mexico DF	URNG–government agreement for freezing of PACs and investigation of their conduct; existing PACs to remain; new ones permitted in event of rebel offensive.

aftermath of the Salvadorean offensive, US Ambassador Thomas Stoock signalled in unusually blunt language the need for improvement in the human rights position. In February 1990, immediately after the Nicaraguan election, Stoock declared, 'it is impossible for the US to maintain stable and enduring relations with a government that violates human rights'.[219] A few days later he was officially withdrawn because of the continuing failure of the military and the death squads to curb their activities just as Ramiro de León Carpio (appointed in December 1989) began to make the office of ombudsman politically important with his detailed reports and direct language. The European Community had already made improvements in human rights a condition of aid, and for several years this issue had caused much-publicized embarrassment for the government in the UN. The unambiguous signal from Washington early in 1990 that it would no longer accept weasel words encouraged the Cerezo regime to authorize a further meeting with the guerrillas by the CNR although it would not itself hazard a repetition of the Madrid encounter.

This stand-off continued for the next twelve months. Washington's pressure was maintained by very public protests at the lack of action over the murder of US citizen Michael Devine by soldiers in the Petén in June 1990. The massacre by troops in December of some twenty unarmed villagers in Santiago Atitlán hardened the resolve of the US Congress to cut economic aid, which was much greater than that to the military, and this decision was ratified early in 1991. Furthermore, the election of Jorge Serrano in January 1991 to replace Cerezo as president did not have the same effect on Washington as had that of Cristiani in El Salvador in 1989; there was a much more cautious reaction beneath the expressions of goodwill. Further fierce and public criticisms of the human rights situation by the UN (February 1991) and the US State Department (January 1992) ensured that this would remain central to outside pressure on the regime to treat with its enemies and to the substance of any negotiations.

For its part, the URNG, which lacked the confidence and dexterity of the Sandinistas and FMLN, registered some political success by exploiting the Cerezo government's reluctance to talk and holding international meetings with representatives of major social groups. That held with the entrepreneurs' confederation CACIF in September promised to erode the military veto and government timidity, but the rebels continued to insist on a full set of economic demands that were plainly unacceptable to the capitalists. This, it might be remembered, was before the FMLN had entered into serious talks with the Salvadorean regime and reduced their focus to transitional political arrangements and the question of human rights. By contrast, the Guatemalan guerrillas insisted throughout on retaining a set of substantive economic demands on their agenda despite their weak position. Nonetheless, the meetings of 1990 enabled Serrano to address the peace question rapidly upon coming to office, and for the first few months of his presidency it appeared that Guatemala was about to undergo a version of the Salvadorean experience whereby a conservative regime that replaced a Christian Democratic administration felt able to talk directly with the rebels.

It is the case that by mid 1991 US pressure, developments elsewhere in the region, and its containment of the URNG had combined to reduce the army's aversion to negotiations. Although much of the commentary on different currents within the military is speculative – and sometimes more an expression of imagination than firm evidence – it seems clear that a good portion of those younger officers who had spent much of the 1980s fighting the guerrillas was not inalterably opposed to formalizing an end to hostilities.[220] Indeed, insofar as the counter-insurgency doctrine represented by Gramajo possessed a strong Clause-witzian strain – albeit through inversion: politics as war by other means – negotiation was not anathema per se. Some senior officers evidently disagreed, but they could no longer enforce their view.

The passage of negotiations in mid 1991 did not, however, give grounds for great optimism after the first round in Mexico, where it proved possible to agree a broad agenda, including socio-economic issues, for future discussions.[221] A second meeting at Querétaro reached a consensus over the broad principles of liberal democracy without undue difficulty. It was, though, once again the issue of human rights that provided the major stumbling-block throughout the autumn, even after the Salvadorean peace agreement had been concluded. For over a year the URNG remained intransigent on its core requirements in this regard – a Truth Commission; reversal of the 1985 amnesty; abolition of the PACs, obligatory military conscription and the paramilitary agencies; government payment of compensation to the victims of repression; and the effective removal of the *fuero militar*, with most crimes committed by military personnel to be assigned to civilian jurisdiction. None of these requirements was acceptable to the military or deemed worthy of serious debate by the government negotiators.

In May 1992 the URNG proposed reducing the scope of discussions by postponing negotiation over the details of a ceasefire, demobilization and legalization of the rebel forces. This initiative succeeded in circumventing the often arid exchanges over preconditions that combined profound rebel fears over security with military insistence on surrender. At the same time, it laid the basis for an agreement over refugee return in October which – despite much criticism from the popular organizations at the time of the awarding of the Nobel Peace Prize to Rigoberta Menchú – was important insofar as it opened channels of exchange between the state and the mass movement, compelling both to engage in a modicum of manoeuvre. On the other hand, the URNG's insistence on a range of economic demands appeared counter-productive. It is the case that the FMLN had been able to include in the Chapultepec accords precise clauses on land distribution together with arrangements for subsequent debate over economic policy. Yet the Salvadorean left had much greater bargaining power, and the land question had offered Cristiani a forum for displaying the merits of 'popular capitalism', whereas talk of agrarian reform was tanta- mount to heresy for the bulk of the Guatemalan elite. Moreover, it appeared that the URNG was insisting on the issue more for propa- ganda purposes than as an item for genuine negotiation, possibly as part of a 'maximum programme' over which concessions could subsequently be made.[222] The impression of a misguidedly prolonged conflation of substantive programme and negotiating platform was reduced some- what by the URNG's clear concession in accepting the freezing rather than abolition of the PACs in August 1992. However, such shifts proceeded more slowly than developments within legal public life, which became increasingly important after Serrano's election and which took on a decisive character in the late spring of 1993.

The crisis opened by Serrano's suspension of the constitution on 25 May 1993 had as its immediate cause the miscalculations made by a populist politician of limited skill and very slight mass following. Both shortcomings distinguished him from the Peruvian President Alberto Fujimori, whose own *autogolpe* in April 1992 against an obstructive congress and judiciary Serrano sought to emulate. In the case of Guatemala, though, the conflict between the executive, legislature and judiciary had little to do with ideological matters or an authentic political impasse, instead having its roots in the collapse of a spoils system that had become impossibly stressed.

This degeneration of the constitutional regime was discernible even under Cerezo in that public administration was widely treated as a source of funds by those who belonged to or now joined a party that had never previously held power in its thirty-year history.[223] After 1991 the problem became much sharper because although Serrano readily beat Jorge Carpio (UCN), winning 68 per cent of the run-off vote, his own MAS party held only 18 of Congress's 103 seats. As a result, Serrano had to enter into alliance with both the DCG and the UCN. In practice this meant ceding control of the Supreme Court to ex-UCN deputy Juan José Rodil, who became its president in January 1992 after a secret congressional election of the nine justices. In November 1992 controversial internal congressional elections, in which the MAS/DCG/ UCN alliance presented a single slate, were won by the DCG deputy Fernando Lobo Dubón who assumed the presidency of the chamber and thereby became a key – and competitive – broker of power and patronage.

Serrano was, then, not quite the unencumbered individualist he liked to project. In January 1991 nearly a million Guatemalans had voted for him in a second-round contest against Carpio, but in the first round of November 1990 Serrano had won less than 400,000 votes. Moreover, his candidacy had benefited enormously from the withdrawal of the populist autocrat General Efrain Rios Montt, who was obliged to step down shortly before the poll because he had led a de facto regime in 1982–83. In April 1990 – when Rios Montt was still in contention – Serrano's standing in the opinion polls was at between 1 and 2 per cent. Once Rios Montt was out, much of his support went to Serrano, who had served in the general's earlier dictatorship, was backed by the same fundamentalist Protestant sects, and struck a similar pose as an honest outsider prepared to assail the vested interests. Instead, once he reached the presidency, Serrano was obliged to join those interests, creating tangible disenchantment. Owing his election in large measure to 'negative voting', he was far more vulnerable than it seemed to popular assessment of his performance as well as to continued backing from his informal allies in the UCN and DCG. Both these factors swung decisively against him in mid May 1993.

The MAS won the municipal elections of 9 May by a margin so great that charges of vote-buying and fraud seemed highly plausible. Furthermore, these accusations were made not only by the small extreme right-wing parties that had earlier protested at the MAS/DCG/UCN triad's carve-up of congressional power. Now they were also levelled by the UCN, which lost nearly a hundred mayoralties, and the DCG, which lost almost fifty while the MAS increased its share from thirteen to 100. Serrano responded by turning against the two main parties the charges of corruption they had raised, in both the Supreme Court and Congress, against him and his closest associates. His 'end game' in this respect was to close Congress down, but the problem was that after nearly two years of collaboration all these groups were involved in overlapping spoils systems, provoking popular repugnance in roughly equal measure.

The details of malfeasance in contemporary Guatemala are distinctly lurid, corruption almost constituting a political economy of its own. However, for our purposes it will serve to note that Serrano and his vice-president Gustavo Espina were publicly identified in March 1993 as having acquired property worth at least $20 million since their election. At that time the governor of the department of Izabal fled into exile, having accused Serrano's cousins of taking over a state farm, and it transpired that the deeds to the president's two new farms were irregular.[224] Naturally, such matters played directly into the hands of his opponents. They, though, were hardly less vulnerable. In the case of Congress one of the principal sources of wealth had become the acquisition of cars stolen in Texas and irregularly provided with congressional plates that provided immunity. This highly profitable activity was closely associated with the veteran PR deputy Obdulio Chinchilla, who dominated the department of Chiquimula, but most other parties were involved too.[225] It was, moreover, one of several cases being pursued with unusual zeal by the attorney general, Acisclo Valladares Molina. The deputies involved naturally invoked their constitutional rights to immunity from prosecution which could only be removed by a vote of two-thirds of the Congress. However, it was not long before Valladares himself became the target of accusations – that he was attempting to bamboozle his 91-year-old aunt into letting him control her $5 million fortune.[226] The attorney general, who was himself protected by immunity clauses but kept true to his prior invectives against impunity, requested that he be investigated and was promptly removed from office by congressional vote. Early in 1993 his replacement, Edgar Tuna, issued strong declarations in favour of the amnesty for the military and attempted to cut back the powers of Ombudsman de León Carpio.

Full details of corruption at Rodil Peralta's Supreme Court were not publicized until after the failure of Serrano's coup, although the court's election in January 1992 was widely attacked as being a purely political exercise. Moreover, the court's reputation was not enhanced either by Rodil's appointment of his nephew as a 'special adviser' or his payment to some twenty secretaries of salaries of over $3,750 a month – more than the basic pay of a congressional deputy.[227] The fact that the Supreme Court had spent $51,000 on weaponry was rather more sinister than Rodil's $4,000 per month petrol bill, but these and other revelations contributed to a general ambience of dishonesty, greatly weakening the charges Rodil and his associates sought to make against the president. In sum, all the main institutions of the state had become badly tarnished and lacked legitimacy.

This fact undoubtedly gave impetus to the popular mobilization against Serrano's announcement of price rises for electricity, fuel and transport immediately after the municipal elections. Although the UCN and DCG – which had earlier helped Serrano evade a congressional debate over the budget – opportunistically attacked these measures, the level of mass protest was quite remarkable for a country so long subjected to violent repression. The demonstrations soon turned into riots with school students burning buses and giving the strong impression that the capital's youth had made a generational turn against the culture of caution and survivalist acquiescence. Its eruption into the streets in mid May 1993 and the resulting police repression provided Serrano with the justification for his coup attempt, but his stock was so low that even within the military arguments over public order were now placed in a wider context of economic policy and public propriety. This was also true of the response of CACIF, which had often criticized the management of the state electricity corporation INDE, held responsible for frequent interruptions of supply and price rises, although the entrepreneurs were far from enthusiastic about paying the taxes to finance the $30,000 daily subsidy needed to keep the capital's bus fares within reach of schoolchildren and the poor.[228]

The failure over fifteen years of both military and civilian governments to manage the provision of fuel, power and transport without provoking riots (1978; 1985; 1990; 1993) might be seen as vindication of the URNG's policy of insisting upon the inclusion of economic policy in the peace negotiations. Furthermore, it should be borne in mind that the price of insubordination in the countryside was markedly higher than in Guatemala City, and the land question clearly had lost none of its edge. It would, though, be misconceived to see the crisis of May and June 1993 predominantly in this light. Whilst, of course, the moral economy of the urban poor related powerfully to the issue of the legitimacy of even a quasi-authoritarian state such as that in constitutional Guatemala, this was more directly affected by the question of violence, especially by the army, police and the death squads associated with them and the groups of the extreme right. For this reason alone a conservative member of the political establishment such as Ramiro de León Carpio was able to become a popular champion because, as ombudsman, he represented both honest conduct and the repudiation of violence.

The collapse of Serrano's dictatorial experiment and the installation of de León Carpio's ad hoc technocratic administration may herald the advent of modernity in Guatemalan politics. This was evident, for example, in the ombudsman's use of a cellphone to organize opposition as he hid from Serrano's goons. It may also be seen in the style and approach of Guatemala's newest daily, *Siglo XXI*, and it may yet prove to be a facet of the army officers who filled the senior military appointments once the new administration found its feet and flushed away the generals who first tried clumsily to hem it in. The obstacles, however, remained formidable. At the Supreme Court, Rodil clung to his post and attempted to dodge a purge by presenting his own, self-serving plans for reform. Lobo Dubón's Congress likewise held out against a popular campaign – led by the unprecedentedly broad Instancia Nacional de Consenso (INC) – for mass resignations, and in the midst of that dispute the UCN leader Jorge Carpio was assassinated, quite possibly by forces on the right.[229]

The historical foundations for pessimism were strong and deep. Yet history also provides a countervailing example in that although Guatemala was the Central American country most emphatically affected by the Cold War, this had been as a result of the overthrow of a decade-long reformist enterprise (1944–54) that had been begun by strongly legalist popular mobilization and had only been destroyed with powerful assistance from the US. The memory of the governments of Arévalo and Arbenz had been dimmed by age and the wrenching brutality of nearly four decades. Contemporary historians have also revealed enough to puncture any easy depiction of a golden age.[230] Nonetheless, that experience, together with the events of mid 1993, must be pitted against the bleak determinism encouraged by the long counter-revolution.

Notes

1. *Central American Report* (hereafter CAR), Guatemala City, 5 Oct. 1990.

2. Pedantry is quite trendy at present, but I think there is good reason to dwell briefly on the use of this word. 'Words in the New World seem always to be trailing after events that pursue a terrible logic quite other than the fragile meanings that they construct. But if we are thus forced to abandon the dream of linguistic omnipotence, the fantasy that to understand the discourse is to understand the event, we are not at the same time compelled or even permitted to discard words altogether ... The possession of weapons and the will to use them on defenceless people are cultural matters that are intimately bound up with discourse, with the stories that a culture tells itself, its conceptions of personal boundary and liability, its whole collective system of rules.' Stephen Greenblatt, *Marvelous Possessions: The Wonder of the New World*, Oxford 1991, pp. 63–4.

3. *Enciclopedia Universal Ilustrada Europeo-Americana*, Madrid 1919, vol. 40, pp. 1331–3.

4. *Ordenanzas de nuevos descubrimientos y poblaciones*, ch. XXIX. Even in Cortés's usage the word is by no means a simple euphemism and embodies important elements of concession, as illustrated by this passage from his 'third letter' of May 1522:

> Dos días antes de Navidad llegó el capitán con la gente de pie y de caballo que habían ido a las provincias de Cecatami y Xalazingo, y supe cómo algunos naturales de ellas habían peleado con ellos, y que al cabo, de ellos por voluntad, de ellos por fuerza, habían venido de paz, y trajéronme algunos señores de aquellas provincias, a los cuales, no embargante que eran muy dignos de culpa por su alzamiento y muertes de cristianos, y porque me prometieron que de ahí adelante serían buenos y leales vasallos de su majestad, yo, en su real nombre, los perdoné y los envié a su tierra; y así se concluyó aquella jornada, en que vuestra majestad fué muy servido, así por la pacificación de los naturales de allí ...

Manuel Alcalá, ed., *Hernán Cortés. Cartas de Relación*, Madrid 1988, p. 105. For Las Casas's usage, see, amongst the many versions recycled throughout his long campaign, *Historia de las Indias*, ch. CXXIV, which directly addresses the use of the word 'conquest', and *Memorial al Consejo de Indias*, which contrasts conquest with 'pacific possession of lands'. Most illustrations of the verb *pacificar* that I have seen relate to non-Europeans and suggest some infantilization of still dangerous people – a sense that is, perhaps, preserved by North American usage of the word 'pacifier' for a baby's dummy. However, one should not forget the utterly unambiguous manner in which the word has been used in the present age, as, for example, in 1971 by Colonel Carlos Arana, President of Guatemala: 'If it is necessary to turn the country into a cemetery in order to pacify it, I will not hesitate to do so.' *New York Times*, 8 May 1971, cited in Jim

Handy, *Gift of the Devil. A History of Guatemala*, Toronto 1984, p. 167.

5. John A. Peeler, 'Democracy and Elections in Central America. Autumn of the Oligarchs?', in John A. Booth and Mitchell Seligson, eds., *Elections and Democracy in Central America*, Chapel Hill 1989, p. 198. A fuller and useful 'ideal type' condensed by Louis Goodman from Linz, Lipset and Diamond runs thus:

> ... a political system with three essential characteristics: (1) meaningful and extensive competition among individuals and organized groups for effective positions of government power at regular intervals that exclude the use of force; (2) a high level of political participation in the selection of leaders, at least through regular and fair elections, such that no major group is excluded; and (3) a level of civil and political liberties – freedom of expression, press, association, assembly – sufficient to ensure the integrity of political competition and participation.

Louis W. Goodman, 'Political Parties and the Political Systems of Central America', in Louis W. Goodman, William M. Leogrande and Johanna Mendelson Forman, eds., *Political Parties and Democracy in Central America*, Boulder 1992, p. 4. Goodman is here compressing slightly a passage on p. xvi of Larry Diamond, Juan K. Linz and Seymour Martin Lipset, eds., *Democracy in Developing Countries: Latin America*, Boulder 1989, which includes only Costa Rica from Central America. For an indication of the problems involved in analysing such matters, see Paul Cammack's explanation of why he feels that the most striking characteristic of this latter volume is 'the contrast between its mighty theoretical aims, and minimal achievements' in *The Journal of International Development*, vol. 3, no. 5, 1991.

6. Richard Fagen, 'The Politics of Transition', in R. Fagen, C. Deere and J.L. Corragio, eds., *Transition and Development*, New York 1986, p. 258.

7. For a lucid and compelling account, see Bhikhu Parekh, 'The Cultural Particularity of Liberal Democracy', in David Held, ed., *Prospects for Democracy*, Oxford 1993.

8. Robert Putnam, *Making Democracy Work: Civic Traditions in Modern Italy*, Princeton 1993.

9. The *Independent*, London, 10 June 1993. It is perhaps unsurprising that Museveni permitted the restoration of the titular kingship of Buganda a few weeks later.

10. Adam Przeworski, 'Some Problems in the Study of the Transition to Democracy', in G. O'Donnell, P. Schmitter and L. Whitehead, eds., *Transitions from Authoritarian Rule. Comparative Perspectives*, Baltimore 1986, p. 58. This statement is, for instance, reproduced at the head of the introductory chapter to Booth and Seligson, *Elections and Democracy*.

11. Kalman Silvert, *Man's Power. A Biased Guide to Political Thought and Action*, New York 1970, quoted in Goodman et al., *Political Parties*, p. 47.

12. Michel de Montaigne, 'That it is madness to judge the true and the false from our own capacities', in *The Complete Essays*, ed. M. Screech, London 1993, p. 200.

13. Elisabeth Burgos-Debray, ed., *I ... Rigoberta Menchú. An Indian Woman in Guatemala*, London 1984, contains this telling statement: 'Indians have been very careful not to disclose any details of their communities, and the community does not allow them to talk about Indian things ... we keep a lot of things to ourselves and the community doesn't like us telling its secrets. This applies to all our customs' (p. 9).

14. Laurence Whitehead, 'The Alternatives to "Liberal Democracy": a Latin American Perspective', in *Political Studies*, vol. XL, 1992, reprinted in Held, ed., *Prospects for Democracy*, pp. 312–29.

15. Rodolfo Cerdas, *El Desencanto Democrático*, San José 1993, p. 21.

16. It should be stressed that O'Donnell's model for the origins and characteristics of bureaucratic authoritarianism has long been the subject of revision and debate, some of it quite heated. For a fair depiction of how it stood at the end of the 1970s, see David Collier, 'Overview of the Bureaucratic Authoritarian Model', in Collier, ed., *The New Authoritarianism in Latin America*, Princeton 1979. Marcelo Cavarozzi has recently

revived the now unfashionably structuralist strain of political interpretation developed by O'Donnell: 'Beyond Transitions to Democracy in Latin America', *Journal of Latin American Studies*, vol. 24, part 2, Oct. 1992.

17. *The Times*, London, 1 May 1989.

18. The *Guardian*, London, 27 May 1993.

19. Whitehead, 'Alternatives to "Liberal Democracy"'. Part of the abstract for his article reads: 'Although current fiscal crises lend some plausibility to the "neo-liberal" analysis of democratization, the paper argues that in the longer run consolidated democracies will tend to develop a range of "social democratic", participatory and interventionist features that are at variance with the neo-liberal model.' Whitehead's references for neo-liberal arguments include A. Krueger, 'The Political Economy of the Rent-Seeking Society', *American Economic Review*, vol. 64, no. 3, 1974; R. Findlay and J. Wilson, 'The Political Economy of Leviathan', in A. Razin and E. Sadka, eds., *Economic Policy in Theory and Practice*, New York 1987; H. de Soto, *The Other Path: the Invisible Revolution in the Third World*, London 1989.

20. I have explored this theme a little more fully in 'Reflections on the Nicaraguan Election', *New Left Review*, no. 182, Aug./Sept. 1990.

21. James Petras and Morris Morley, *Latin America in the Time of Cholera*, London 1992, pp. 128, 129. The authors later list six 'powerful lessons' of the Nicaraguan experience amongst which are: 'third, revolutionary pluralist-socialist democracy either establishes the boundaries for political activity or it self-destructs', and, 'sixth, the consolidation of state and regime power (the elimination of armed external enemies and their internal allies) and the processes of economic reconstruction and development are the *essential prerequisites* of open and democratic elections in Third World revolutionary societies'. Ibid., p. 141. I'm not sure what Petras and Morley are really saying here, but I have every reason to believe them to be honest men, and so must simply accept that I cannot get beyond the evident contradictions in these slogans.

22. In one of their several sharp criticisms of Latin American intellectuals and think-tanks that are in receipt of foreign cash and which 'respond to the political/ideological power of capital' (ibid., p. 154), Petras and Morley launch an eminently quotable 'double-whammy' on Ernesto Laclau: 'If one can cut through the gibberish ("the infinite intertextuality of emancipatory discourses in which the plurality of the social takes place"), Laclau's emphasis on "collective wills", amorphous social groupings, and disembodied democracy is a throwback to his earlier Peronist intellectual formation. In both instances crude national/populist formulations paper over antagonistic class interests.' (Ibid., p. 173, fn 1.) Laclau's language has never been easy however one rates the ideas he has developed over the last fifteen years. Petras and Morley, though, are not entirely beyond a little criticism themselves: 'The repositioning of exploitation into the realm of distribution conflates the positions of labour and capital in production, and this becomes the formula for the policies of class collaboration and "social contracting": both are interdependent "productive factors" in producing income.' (Ibid., p. 149.) The fact is that, if one sits down with a nice cup of tea, it is possible to distil some sense from both assertions, and both have something useful to say. Petras and Morley's observation about Laclau's past is also insightful, but it rather looks as if Petras has decided to let polemic run over into *ad hominem* attacks. In a recent exchange with Carlos Vilas (also an expatriate Argentine), again over the role of intellectuals – an exchange in which Vilas does not possess a complete monopoly of fair points – Petras rejects 'his Stalinist approach of sending critical memos to elites while publicly promoting state policies harmful to popular interests ... Above all, Vilas is a nationalist ideologue against the left.' Petras, meanwhile, belongs to 'the internationalist left'. *Latin American Perspectives*, no. 77, spring 1993, p. 110. One is put in mind of the title of an article written for *Pravda* in April 1923 by Leon Trotsky, arguably as internationalist as James Petras: 'Civility and Politeness as a Necessary Lubricant in Daily Relations'.

23. Of the fifty-seven references to El Salvador – twenty-three of them on 'violence' – in *Deterring Democracy*, London 1991, just four mention the operations of the opposition FMLN, which was engaged in a civil war for ten years. In each of these four

cases the rebels' activities is mentioned as a prelude to a critical observation on the role of the local forces of repression or the USA. It is telling that in this 421-page book Chomsky several times refers to the assassination of the six Jesuit priests in El Salvador in November 1989 but never once mentions that this occurred at the height of an offensive by the FMLN that decisively shifted the local balance of forces as well as Washington's attitude to the conflict. *Year 501. The Conquest Continues*, London 1993, adopts very much the same approach, and, as the title suggests, scarcely hesitates to question the nature of its inquiry. For a buoyant defence of Chomsky's work in general, see Christopher Hitchens, *Prepared for the Worst*, London 1989, pp. 58–77.

24. Jean Piaget, *Structuralism*, London 1971, p. 83.

25. *Year 501*, p. 51.

26. Chomsky's use of contemporary press and secondary sources is extensive, but he does depend very heavily upon the US press at the same time as he often (and properly) criticizes it for bias and partiality, as, for example, in *Deterring Democracy*, p. 174. The absence of any significant countervailing material, and heavy reliance on secondary or tertiary accounts in Chomsky's work, may well be justified in terms of the exceptionally narrow political scope of the US media, but it remains deeply unsatisfying in terms of developing a perspective beyond pure denunciation. For Chomsky's own view, in an interview, see James Peck, ed., *The Chomsky Reader*, London 1987, pp. 1–56.

27. CAR, 24 Feb. 1989, provides a useful summary background on the revolutionary left.

28. Booth and Seligson, *Elections and Democracy*, p. 166.

29. CAR, 28 Sept. 1990.

30. Movimiento Popular de Liberación, or Cinchoneros, established in March 1980; Fuerzas Populares Revolucionarias Lorenzo Zelaya (FPR), 1980; Frente Morazanista de Liberación Nacional (FMLH), 1979; Partido Revolucionario Centroamericano de Trabajadores (PRTC), 1979. CAR, 25 May 1990, gives a brief summary.

31. Cerdas, *Desencanto Democrático*, pp. 125ff.

32. Consejo Monetario Centroamericano, *Boletín Estadístico 1991*, San José 1991; CEPAL, *Preliminary Overview of the Latin American and Caribbean Economy, 1992*, nos. 537/538, Dec. 1992; Interamerican Development Bank, *Economic and Social Progress in Latin America*, Washington 1992.

33. CAR, 20 Dec. 1991.

34. Ibid., 5 Oct. 1989.

35. Ibid., 20 Dec. 1991; 22 Jan. 1993; 13 Nov. 1992. These figures were broadly the same as the previous year's.

36. Ibid., 18 Sept. 1992.

37. Ibid., 7 July 1989. Central American production in the early 1990s was fourteen million quintals; that of Colombia sixteen million; Brazil twenty-one million; and Indonesia seven million.

38. Ibid., 14 May 1993.

39. Ibid., 1 Nov. 1991. Between 1989 and 1991 the price fell from $123 to $85 per quintal.

40. Ibid., 29 June 1993.

41. Ibid., 23 Nov. 1990.

42. Ibid., 17 Jan. 1992.

43. Ibid., 23 April 1993. Over this period Costa Rica was consistently the largest exporter whilst El Salvador remained a late developer.

44. *The Economist*, 26 June 1993. Guatemala's *maquila* exports rose from $39.6 million in 1987 to $451 million in 1992.

45. These and other matters are fully discussed in Victor Bulmer-Thomas, Rodolfo Cerdas, Eugenia Gallardo and Mitchell Seligson, *Central American Integration. Report for the Commission of the European Community*, Miami 1992.

46. CAR, 3 March 1989; 11 Aug. 1989.

47. Ibid., 19 March 1993.

48. Ibid., 13 Sept. 1991.

49. Ibid., 29 June 1990.

50. Ibid., 2 Feb. 1992; 13 March 1992.

51. Ibid., 21 Aug. 1992; 4 Dec. 1992, IPM, owned by the armed forces, showed more than slight interest in buying HONDUTEL, arguing that this was necessary for 'national security'. Such a stirring call has, of course, nothing to do with the fact that HONDUTEL's 1992 profits were reported to be $44 million whilst the IHHS public health system, for which the military did not tender despite its coverage of 900,000 citizens of the Republic, had a deficit of $63 million and was owed $28 million by the government itself. Ibid., 27 Sept. 1991; 2 April 1993. In August 1992 military commander General Discua declared: 'the IPM has ventured into the field of private enterprise and we will defend our right to invest. We are Hondurans and here we are going to clarify that this capital is not the Armed Forces' but the IPM's.' *La Tribuna*, Tegucigalpa, 3 Aug. 1992, quoted in ibid., 16 Oct. 1992.

52. ARENA began its campaign to privatize INCAFE, the state coffee-trading corporation, in October 1988, when it was opposed in Congress by the conservative PCN as well as by the PDC. The coffee entrepreneurs' organization ABECAFE openly sponsored the ARENA proposals, claiming that INCAFE depressed prices and owed some $140 million to the central bank. Ibid., 11 Nov. 1988.

53. Ibid., 13 Oct. 1989; 20 April 1990. Of the banks only the two most stable – the Banco Agrario Comercial and the Banco Cuscatlán – were sold outright, and with limits on stocks available to institutions as a gesture to the notion of popular capitalism; the others were merged or closed. Ibid., 19 July 1991; 13 Dec. 1991. The privatization of the outpatients' services at San Salvador's central hospital run by the Instituo Salvadoreño de Seguridad Social in August 1990 was extended in mid 1991 with the introduction of charges. Ibid., 31 Aug. 1990; 27 Sept. 1991. The large demonstration organized by INTERGREMIAL on 29 August 1991 against privatization may well have tempered government ambitions.

54. Ibid., 13 Dec. 1991.

55. Ibid., 19 March 1993.

56. CEPAL, *Preliminary Overview ... 1992*, p. 41.

57. CAR, 20 July 1990; CEPAL, *Preliminary Overview ... 1992*, passim. Nicaragua's illiteracy rate was better than the Latin American average.

58. CAR, 8 Nov. 1991, citing *Envío*.

59. *La Nación*, San José, 28 July 1992 and 3 Aug. 1992, cited in Cerdas, *Desencanto Democrático*, pp. 129–30.

60. CAR, 27 March 1992.

61. Ibid.

62. For a good general survey of Latino immigrant culture and politics in the USA, see NACLA, *Report on the Americas*, vol. XXVI, nos. 1 and 2, July/Sept. 1992. For a marvellous pot-pourri of US/Salvadorean/Latino cultural exchanges, see Rubén Martínez, *The Other Side*, London 1992. The Salvadorean presence in what seems to some to be the inferno of Los Angeles is properly recognized in Mike Davis's masterly accounts: *City of Quartz*, London 1990; 'Who Killed Los Angeles?', *New Left Review*, no. 197, 1993; and 'Los Angeles on Trial', *New Left Review*, no. 199, 1993.

63. ILO, cited in CAR, 21 Oct. 1988.

64. Ibid., 27 Oct. 1989.

65. Ibid., 19 March 1993. By contrast, the figure for Costa Rica, where 70 per cent of sexually active women use contraception, is statistically insignificant.

66. Ibid., 23 Nov. 1990; 26 March 1993.

67. Ibid., 13 Dec. 1991; 30 April 1993. Hugh O'Shaughnessy's extensive article in the *Observer*, London, 26 Sept. 1993, showed the position in Guatemala and El Salvador to be similar, if not worse.

68. Honduras experienced 143 deaths and disappearances due to political persecution and violence between 1979 and 1986 – almost all of them between 1982 and 1984, when the armed forces were controlled by General Alvarez Martínez, a man sharply

inclined to repression and who was assassinated, probably by the Cinchoneros, in January 1989.

69. For a committed but compelling account of her capture in 1984 with a few telling observations on gender relations as well as the early phase of talks between the FMLN and the state, see Nidia Díaz, *I Was Never Alone. A Prison Diary from El Salvador*, Melbourne 1992.

70. Lea Guido, minister of health; Daisy Zamora, deputy minister of culture; and the late Nora Astorga, deputy foreign minister. The leading female Sandinista military figure, Dora María Tellez, was vice-president of the Council of State.

71. Daniel Ortega, 'Informe Central de la Dirección Nacional del FSLN', Managua 1991, p. 21.

72. Lisa Haugaard, 'With and Against the State. Organizing Dilemmas for Grass-roots Movements in Nicaragua', Columbia University, Conference Paper no. 54, April 1991, pp. 17–18.

73. Gerald Martin, *Journeys through the Labyrinth. Latin American Fiction in the Twentieth Century*, London 1989, p. 366.

74. In March 1832 the British Tory MP Spencer Perceval associated the recent epidemic with the passage of the Great Reform Bill. Cholera had been 'hanging over the country as a curse from the first day on which the Bill had been introduced, and a curse it hath been upon the country from that time to this'. Quoted in Asa Briggs, *The Age of Improvement, 1783–1867*, London 1959, p. 254, fn 1. Cholera also struck Britain on the eve of reform legislation and disturbances in Ireland in 1866, prompting Briggs to call it 'the regular harbinger of political excitement'. (Ibid., p. 504.) The invasion of cholera into Guatemala and Nicaragua in 1836 clearly abetted the Conservative offensive against the post-independence Liberal regimes in the isthmus. There is a far less clear political link for the epidemic of 1856, which struck Costa Rica, El Salvador and Honduras, although the last occurrence of the disease in each of those countries was in 1871 – the year of the strong Liberal resurgence. Panamerican Health Organization, *Epidemological Bulletin*, vol. 12, no. 1, 1992.

75. Snow overturned prevailing medical theory which held cholera to be caused by the inhalation of 'miasma', poisonous vapours given off by rotting rubbish and excrement. As a result of this view, much effort was expended in watering streets and flushing sewers to clear stagnant waste – actions which only spread the disease further. Snow carefully mapped the distribution of cases in the outbreaks of 1848–49 and 1853–54, and in one case-study of Soho was able to demonstrate that a single well in Broad Street was the cause of infection.

76. CAR, 9 Aug. 1991; *Newsweek*, 6 May 1991.

77. CAR, 24 Jan. 1992.

78. Ibid., 22 May 1992. By November 1992 Central America had registered over 33,000 cases of cholera (5,810 of them in 1991 and 18,090 in Guatemala alone) and 423 deaths (105 in 1991). In the first few months Nicaragua suffered a sharp increase in cases, leading to 24 deaths, whilst Guatemala was able to keep the infection under control with only 326 new cases and 3 deaths. In the view of the World Health Organization cholera is 'under control' if deaths are less than one per cent of cases. This was true of all countries except Panama (1,211 cases and 31 deaths by January 1992).

79. Honduras, with a population of only five million, has registered 2,212 cases of AIDS and 654 deaths since 1985. This not only makes it by far the most seriously affected Central American country but also constitutes the third-highest rate of incidence in Latin America after Brazil and Mexico. Of these cases 77 per cent are said to be of heterosexuals, but Tegucigalpa's attention was called to International AIDS Day in 1992 by the country's first ever gay demonstration. Ibid., 29 Jan. 1993.

80. Ibid., 11 May 1990; 13 June 1990.

81. Ibid., 28 July 1989.

82. Ibid., 15 Sept. 1989.

83. Ibid., 2 April 1993 (which also quotes the criticism of the entrepreneurial spokesman Adolfo Facussé); Cerdas, *Desencanto Democrático*, pp. 42–3. Rodolfo

Cerdas has memorably remarked that the military's ownership of a funeral parlour gave them a monopoly of both supply and demand in that quarter. *Central America after the Crisis*, Institute of Latin American Studies, University of London, Conference Papers, December 1992, p. 9.

84. Cerdas, *Desencanto Democrático*, p. 27; CAR, 8 Nov. 1991. One telling instance of the degree of professionalism prevailing in the Honduran military is given by the seven-month delay in the promotion of sixty officers, including six colonels, who had failed their exams in December 1991. General Discua was eventually obliged to authorize the promotions after prolonged pressure and accusations that the Armed Forces Superior Council (CONSUFFAA) had deliberately made the papers too difficult. Ibid., 14 Aug. 1992.

85. Ibid., 28 April 1989; 30 June 1989; 27 July 1990; 14 June 1991. For the increased movement of weapons in Costa Rica, see ibid., 5 Oct. 1990.

86. The *Tico Times*, San José, 30 April; 7 May; 14 May 1993. Guillermo 'Charlie' Fallas, thirty-two, was fired from the OIJ in 1990 for participating in an illegal raid on a bar. He claimed that the government had denied him a disability pension for his cirrhosis, and he staged the kidnap with his brother, Gilberto, a jailer for the OIJ, his uncle, Sergio, a retired security guard, and two friends who were also security guards. Despite being what was by Costa Rican standards an unusually well-armed and trained group, the kidnappers were easily tricked into surrendering when they arrived at the airport and expected to collect the ransom. This operation was directed by the country's 'only official soldier', sixty-year-old Alfonso J. Ayub, who saw action in the 1948 civil war and then joined the US Army before returning to set up a hydraulic parts business in San José. A part-time specialist in capturing hijackers, Ayub told the *Tico Times*, 'I don't like to use force unless it's absolutely necessary.'

87. CAR, 24 Jan. 1992; 13 March 1992. One notes a similar pattern in Panama after the invasion. In 1992 there were 53 reported homicides; 3,000 armed robberies; 10,000 thefts; and 3,000 thefts of cars, despite the expansion of the police force to 9,000 officers and the existence in the capital of 156 security firms. Ibid., 15 Feb. 1993.

88. In October 1990 members of the EPS were obliged by foreign pressure to desist from selling twenty SAM missiles to the FMLN. In October 1991 nineteen people were tried for stealing 20 missiles, 600 grenades and 39 rocket-launchers, valued at over $900,000. In May 1993 police uncovered a cache of 19 SAM-7 and SAM-14 missiles and 170 guns in Managua belonging to the FPL; at the end of the month a large explosion revealed a much more extensive armoury. Ibid., 1 Nov. 1991; 11 June 1993; 18 June 1993. According to ONUSAL, by mid June 1993 the total FMLN arsenal retrieved from Nicaragua amounted to 2,268 guns; 6 machine-guns; 281 grenade-launchers; 81 rockets; 21 mortars; 55 light artillery weapons; and 19 missiles.

89. Ibid., 5 March 1993.

90. Ibid., 16 Aug. 1991.

91. Ibid., 19 June 1992.

92. Although it is now ten years old – and has been overtaken by many events – there is still much to be gained from a reading of Laurence Whitehead, 'Explaining Washington's Central American Policies', *Journal of Latin American Studies*, vol. 15, part 2, 1983.

93. William Leogrande, 'From Reagan to Bush: the Transition in US Policy towards Central America', *Journal of Latin American Studies*, vol. 22, part 3, 1990, p. 599. I have relied heavily on this lucid exposition for the following paragraphs. For a detailed study of the Reagan period, see Roy Gutman, *The Making of American Policy in Nicaragua, 1981–1987*, New York 1988.

94. Leogrande, 'From Reagan to Bush', p. 599.

95. The full accord is reprinted in CAR, 7 April 1989.

96. In late November 1989 the House voted 215–194 against a proposal to withhold 30 per cent of the $85 million approved for fiscal year 1990, and the Senate followed suit.

97. The victory of Cristiani in March 1989 had prompted considerable disquiet in

Washington, not least, of course, because it had consumed a portion of its propaganda demonizing ARENA to the benefit of the Christian Democrats (most specifically, in previous years, José Napoleón Duarte). However, the close association of Roberto D'Aubuissón with both the death squads and the party, and the conviction that Cristiani was little more than a stooge for the squads, gave sharper edge to the disquiet. The newly ensconced Bush administration was, though, also to obtain a House vote of 233–185 to keep military aid free of conditions. In the Senate the conversion of Dodd, following a meeting with a new Salvadorean president, produced an even more convincing margin of 68–32, but if the consensus had been buoyed up in June 1989 thanks to Dodd, he was correspondingly able to turn the tables a year later. Leogrande, 'From Reagan to Bush', p. 608.

98. CAR, 26 Oct. 1990.

99. Leogrande, 'From Reagan to Bush', p. 618.

100. The *Guardian*, London, 30 Dec. 1989. The music included 'I Fought the Law and the Law Won' (Bobby Fuller Four); 'Beat It' (Michael Jackson); 'You're No Good' (Linda Ronstadt); and 'Let's Dance' (David Bowie). The nuncio, Monsignor Juan Sebastián Laboa, failed to sleep for three nights, and the Vatican's pleas eventually halted the din. It is, of course, the case that a profoundly demoralized Noriega gave himself up soon thereafter, but against this rather questionable achievement should be set the scorn expressed abroad at such a spectacle. Perhaps it is no coincidence that President Bush, whose image was scarcely that of a thug, was at the time absent from Washington, on a holiday quail-hunting.

101. John Weeks and Phil Gunson, *Panama. Made in the USA*, London 1991, pp. 10–11; the *Guardian*, 1 Jan. 1990.

102. The *Guardian*, 1 Jan. 1990. For a text that recycles such charges with minimal qualification, see R.M. Koster and Guillermo Sánchez Borbon, *In the Time of the Tyrants. Panama, 1968–1989*, London 1990.

103. Noriega's bisexuality was evident but barely scandalous in any but the most oligarchic circles of Panamanian society. Even the energetic US propagandists were rather coy about trying to exploit this, tending instead to concentrate upon the case of homosexual rape that was never shown to be more than a rumour. Frederick Kempe, *Divorcing the Dictator*, London 1990, p. 39. Noriega was linked with several cases of rape and, despite the fact that he was out of the country at the time, must be held directly accountable for the appalling manner in which Hugo Spadafora was tortured and murdered in September 1985. Noriega and his long-time associate Colonel Roberto Díaz both consulted psychics. Ibid., pp. 209ff. So also, of course, did Nancy Reagan.

104. Kempe, *Divorcing the Dictator*, pp. 123–5. According to the FDP's own projections, the veteran populist Arnulfo Arias had a lead of some 66,000 votes over the vice-president of the World Bank and Chicago PhD Ardito Barletta. Secretary of State George Shultz proclaimed himself a friend of the new president; Noriega had chosen his candidate well.

105. The newly appointed Elliott Abrams urged Barletta on the telephone to resist but held back from making an issue of the case. Ibid., p. 156.

106. Ibid., pp. 76–9, 194–205; Weeks and Gunson, *Panama*, pp. 50–51; the *Guardian*, 28 July 1990.

107. Kempe quotes a US official as stating that Washington's self-serving view in the 1970s was that 20 per cent of Noriega's information went to Cuba and 80 per cent to the US. Ibid., p. 112. For Bush's discussions with Noriega, see ibid., pp. 28ff.

108. Ibid., pp. 96, 110, 164ff.

109. Ibid., pp. 176–9.

110. Ibid., p. 180. The argument that US policy in Central America was drug-driven is made, too strongly, in Peter Dale Scott and Jonathan Marshall, *Cocaine Politics. Drugs, Armies and the CIA in Central America*, Berkeley 1991.

111. *New York Times*, 12 June 1986.

112. Kempe, *Divorcing the Dictator*, p. 171.

113. Ibid., p. 121.

114. The nature of the Panamanian crisis of 1987–89 again provides a good opportunity to test the scope of explanation. This ranges from the capacity of a country of less than three million people and without its own currency to survive an eighteen-month dollar boycott by the USA courtesy of the 'workers' states' and off-shore banking interests, to the fact that the final crisis was provoked in June 1987 by Noriega reneging on a deal over promotion with his long-standing acquaintance Colonel Roberto Díaz, against whom he is said to have harboured a grudge since 1959, when Díaz's 'older woman' in Lima spurned Noriega's advances. Ibid., p. 146.

115. Washington Office on Latin America (WOLA), *Clear and Present Dangers. The US Military and the War on Drugs in the Andes*, Washington 1991, p. 76.

116. Even in the late 1980s reported consumption of marijuana and cocaine in Guatemala by those in their twenties was appreciably higher than in Colombia and Mexico. Peter H. Smith, ed., *Drug Policy in the Americas*, Boulder 1992, p. 50.

117. CAR, 5 June 1992; 12 March 1993; the *Independent*, 24 Oct. 1990; *The Economist*, 22 Sept. 1990.

118. CAR, 12 March 1993; *Newsweek*, 29 March 1993. Figures for seizures in the rest of the region were: Belize – 850 kilos of cocaine (13 in 1991) and over 1,000 hectares of marijuana under cultivation; Costa Rica – 2,000 kilos of cocaine, 7 kilos of heroin and 970 rocks of crack; El Salvador – 661 kilos of cocaine; Honduras – 1,500–2,000 kilos of cocaine; Nicaragua – 759 kilos of cocaine. Drugs worth $1.3 million were confiscated between 1985 and 1992 in Guatemala. CAR, 12 March 1993.

119. CAR, 11 Aug. 1989; 11 Oct. 1991; 22 Nov. 1991; Cerdas, *Desencanto Democrático*, p. 171.

120. CAR, 22 Nov. 1991; 5 Oct. 1991; 26 April 1991; 6 July 1990.

121. Kempe, *Divorcing the Dictator*, p. 188.

122. CAR, 8 May 1992.

123. Ibid., 27 Oct. 1989. The 'revelations' were made in the *New York Times*, 15 Oct. 1989. Regalado's predecessor, General Walter López, was accused in July 1986 of stealing $450,000 destined for the Contras. *Honduras Update*, Boston, July 1986.

124. Regalado's brother Rigoberto is serving a ten-year term after being caught in May 1988 with ten kilos of cocaine at Miami airport whilst he was ambassador to Panama. His niece Tania avoided charges of smuggling the drug into Honduras inside electrical appliances, and her husband, Tony Mateo, having been detained in Guatemala and handed over to the US authorities, was eventually released for lack of proof. CAR, 27 Oct. 1989; 12 Jan. 1990. In the case of Guatemalan presidential candidate Alfonso Cabrera the US embassy declared, 'we're not accusing him, but neither can we give him a clean bill of health'. (Ibid., 30 March 1990.) The US also requested the extradition of Elder Vargas, UCN mayor of Zacapa, caught with 3,500 kilos in March 1991.

125. Oduber was accused of receiving 1 million córdobas from Lionel Casey, and he resigned from the PLN whilst the charges were investigated and eventually found to be wanting. Ibid., 28 July 1989; 4 May 1990; 24 Aug. 1990. The PUSC, whose candidate Rafael Calderón won the 1990 presidential election, was alleged to have received $100,000 from the Cuban-American smuggler Lloyd Rubin whilst Calderón's cousin, Carlos Aguilar, was forced to resign over swindles undertaken when he was ambassador to Nicaragua. Ibid., 7 Feb. 1992; 15 Oct. 1991. The fact that the campaign cost the country's two major parties over $30 million – half of which was privately contributed – indicates one of the key areas where constitutional regimes are vulnerable to overtures from *narcotráfico*.

126. *For the Sake of Argument*, London 1993, p. 101. It is worth noting that in the spring of 1993 the PLN very nearly divided over charges of murder made against one of its primary candidates (José María Figueres) by another (José Miguel Corrales) – a matter that might be thought very '*untico*'. CAR, 26 March 1993.

127. Carlos Acevedo, 'El Salvador's New Clothes: The Electoral Process (1982–89)', in Anjali Sundaram and George Gelber, eds., *A Decade of War. El Salvador Confronts the Future*, London 1991, p. 29.

128. Ibid., pp. 143, 162; Cristina Eguizabal, 'Parties, Programs and Politics in El

Salvador', in Goodman et al., *Political Parties*, p. 142.
129. CAR, 18 Aug. 1989.
130. Ibid., 23 Oct. 1992.
131. 'For more than ten years of government the FSLN subscribed to values that were very idealist. We were very schematic and rigid, greatly misled by idealist conceptions, and we did not legitimate practices which are universal. We placed very high value on everything collective or to do with the state, and very low importance on those things to do with the individual – something that experience taught us was completely wrong. After losing the elections we faced a reality in which the new government did not hold this collectivist idealism ... so we hurried to legalize matters, and even ex-President Jimmy Carter advised us to do it legally ... The Sandinistas, who had worked so hard for ten years, with extremely low wages, no free weekends, without cars or houses ... these people were going to be thrown out into the street ... Since Daniel Ortega led a constitutional government we decided to allocate legally the properties in which we lived ...' Quoted in *La Nación*, San José, 22 Sept. 1991, and cited in Cerdas, *Desencanto Democrático*, p. 135.
132. According to Daniel Ortega, 'We gave away as many houses as we could. We gave trucks, cars, forgave outstanding debts, gave away all the construction materials we had warehoused, gave away all the money we could to the families of war casualties and veterans. We gave away everything we could, and in that way protected an important sector of the population and an important sector of the Sandinista rank and file.' Quoted in the *New York Times*, 24 June 1991, and cited in Henry Patterson and Carmel Roulston, 'The Sandinistas in Opposition', *The Journal of Communist Studies*, vol. 8, no. 4, Dec. 1992, p. 234. According to Arce, the FSLN had handed over to the state a Soviet Tu-154 jet worth \$20 million and two Czech radio transmitters in Zelaya, but he had argued with workers that 'it wasn't the same to share out the Victoria de Julio sugar-mill or the San Antonio sugar-mill to the workers as for them to go on being the people's patrimony'. (*Barricada Internacional*, Managua, 5 May 1990.) At the end of his judicious appraisal of the Revolution, Carlos Vilas notes, 'Revolutions are beautiful and seductive because they express what is best and most noble in human beings; the limitless capacity for solidarity and sacrifice to build a life worth living. But they are also terrible because together with these heights of altruism and generosity, there are moments of incredible meanness and small-mindedness, and the great achievements mingle with the most monstrous errors.' ('Nicaragua: a Revolution that Fell from Grace', *Socialist Register 1991*, London 1991, p. 319.)
133. Patterson and Roulston, 'Sandinistas in Opposition', p. 234. The FSLN National Directorate's report to the 1991 Congress made no specific reference to the *piñata* but did refer to the El Crucero document in noting that '(a) some *compañeros* had lifestyles that contrasted with the difficult conditions confronting the majority of our people', and '(b) there were instances of people lacking prestige or accused of corruption who were kept in post or transferred to comparable positions or even promoted'. (*Informe Central*, p. 27.) The Assembly vote, late in March 1990, was 67 votes against 2, with the UNO representatives (elected in November 1984) abstaining. According to Carlos Cuadra, leader of the maoist MAP, 'the first thing they should do is abandon those luxurious houses. I cannot conceive of a revolutionary who would divide up real estate like war booty.' (The *Guardian*, 30 March 1990. See also the *Guardian*, 9 March 1990.) In June 1991 the FSLN temporarily withdrew from the National Assembly in protest at government proposals to revoke Laws 85 and 86.
134. See, for instance, CAR, 16 June 1989; 26 Jan. 1990; 27 Sept. 1991; 1 Nov. 1991.
135. See 'La Corrupción en Honduras, 1982–85', *Boletín Informativo Honduras*, no. 3, Sept. 1985; James Dunkerley, *Power in the Isthmus*, London 1988, pp. 567–8.
136. CAR, 14 April 1989; 9 June 1989; 17 Nov. 1989. Eventually some 70,000 voters were permitted to cast a ballot by presenting their normal ID card. CAR, 12 Jan. 1989.
137. *Power in the Isthmus*, pp. 579–81.

138. CAR, 13 Sept. 1991; 20 Sept. 1991; 28 Feb. 1992; 29 Jan. 1993; 28 May 1993.

139. I am here, of course, deliberately bending a term associated with a school of international relations theory that is state-based, operates on the assumption of irredeemable self-interest, and therefore requires of necessity a balance of power to avoid conflict, as in Hans Morgenthau's *Power among Nations*, New York 1948. The association is obviously inexact, but at least it evokes the East-West and Cold War matrices through which US hegemony, and Central American subordination, were rationalized during most of the 1980s.

140. James Petras, as we have seen, is a prominent advocate of the first position. For the second, see George Vickers, 'A Spider's Web', *NACLA*, vol. XXIV, June 1990; 'Nicaragua: Is the Revolution Over?', Conference Paper no. 50, Graduate Center and Brooklyn College of the City University of New York, April 1991; and William Goodfellow and James Morrell, 'Esquipulas: Politicians in Command', in Goodman et al., *Political Parties*.

141. Washington also ignored a joint Mexican–Venezuelan proposal of September 1982 although Under-Secretary of State Thomas Enders was permitted to hold one meeting of a 'Forum for Peace and Democracy' in October of that year, excluding Guatemala and Nicaragua on the grounds that they were undemocratic. This forum served only as a platform from which to attack Cuba and Nicaragua, alienating several local governments who had anticipated at least a semblance of negotiation.

142. Bruce Bagley, Roberto Alvarez and Katherine J. Hagedorn, eds., *Contadora and the Central American Peace Process. Selected Documents*, Boulder 1985; Adolfo Aguilar Zinser, 'Negotiation in Conflict. Central America and Contadora', in Nora Hamilton, Jeffry A. Frieden, Linda Fuller and Manuel Pastor Jnr, eds., *Crisis in Central America*, Boulder 1988.

143. *Report of the President's National Bipartisan Commission on Central America*, Washington 1984, p. 142.

144. There was a period in mid 1984, during the US election campaign, when the administration appeared to be softening its stance and permitted Secretary of State Shultz to engage in bilateral talks with the FSLN at Manzanillo, Mexico, in June. This overture produced only the offer to reconsider the Nicaraguan case if Soviet and Cuban advisers were expelled. After Reagan's re-election no further talks were held. In January 1986 the core and support groups of Contadora issued the Carabellada Declaration, endorsed by Central American foreign ministers, calling for a halt to Contra aid and a revival of the Contadora proposals. Shultz rejected this, and Reagan refused to receive a delegation.

145. In April 1983 Costa Rica reported Nicaragua to the Organization of American States (OAS) for making armed incursions into its territory, and similar charges were repeatedly made by San José despite clear evidence in the early 1980s that Contra operations were being launched into Nicaragua from Costa Rican territory.

146. This statement would, I believe, be true even if the recent higher estimates of the Central American population at the time of the conquest were correct because much of the subsequent collapse was due to disease. There is also the argument that modern technology of warfare, whilst it might be no less alien and terrifying for the local population than were the horses and gunpowder of the sixteenth century, permits extremely rapid movement of forces and thus extensive disturbance without corresponding engagement. W. George Lovell, 'Surviving Conquest: the Maya of Guatemala in Historical Perspective', *Latin American Research Review*, vol. XXIII, no. 2, 1988; *Conquest and Survival in Colonial Guatemala*, 2nd edn, Montreal 1992; Linda A. Newson, *Indian Survival in Colonial Nicaragua*, Norman, Okl. 1987. For a clear synthesis of the contemporary problem, see CEPAL, *El Impacto Económico y Social de las Migraciones en Centroamérica*, Informe no. 89, Santiago 1993.

147. CAR, 30 Oct. 1992. The Guatemalan refugee experience in the early 1980s is analysed in detail in Beatriz Manz, *Refugees of a Hidden War*, New York 1988.

148. CAR, 21 Aug. 1992.

149. Wilson's point about state insinuation is made in 'Anchored Communities:

Identity and History of the Maya-Q'eqchi'', *Man*, vol. 28, no. 1, 1993. Fuller appraisals of the role of repression are given in his 'Machine-guns and Mountain Spirits', *Critique of Anthropology*, vol. 11, no. 1, 1991, and 'Continued Counter-insurgency: Civilian Rule in Guatemala, 1986–91', in B. Gills, J. Rocamora and R. Wilson, eds., *Low Intensity Democracy: Political Power in the New World Order*, London forthcoming. See also Carol A. Smith, ed., *Guatemalan Indians and the State, 1540–1988*, Austin 1990; and R. Carmack, *Harvest of Violence*, Norman, Okl. 1988.

150. CAR, 29 Nov. 1991.

151. Ibid., 18 Nov. 1988; 1 Dec. 1990; 22 Dec. 1990; 13 March 1992.

152. Cerdas, *Desencanto Democrático*, p. 73.

153. The freezing of aid to Nicaragua by the US Senate vote of 77–23 at the end of July 1993 was justified by the discovery of a large FPL arms cache in Managua following an explosion on 23 May. The vote also occurred after the seizure of Estelí by rebel Sandinista troops on 22 July in an act of desperation that provided demonstration, for all who wished to see, of the cost of withholding funds from the Nicaraguan government.

154. Of the several right-wing religious groups operating in Central America and the USA one might make special mention of the 'Word/City of God' organization because it was said to exercise great influence inside the Chamorro government, and one of its leading figures, Thomas Monaghan, the owner of Domino's Pizza and the Detroit Tigers baseball team, was a major funder of the Contras. For discussion of Protestantism, see David Stoll, *Is Latin America Turning Protestant?*, Berkeley 1990.

155. Costa Rica – PUSC in 1990; El Salvador – ARENA in 1989; Guatemala – MAS in 1991; Honduras – PN in 1989; Nicaragua – UNO in 1990. For an excellent survey, see Rodolfo Cerdas Cruz, Juan Rial and Daniel Zovatto, eds., *Una Tarea Inconclusa. Elecciones y Democracia en América Latina, 1988–1991*, San José 1992.

156. M. Seligson and M. Gomez, 'Ordinary Elections in Extraordinary Times', in Seligson and Booth, *Elections and Democracy*, p. 167.

157. CAR, 16 April 1993.

158. Rodolfo Cerdas stresses the age and experience of political parties. *Desencanto Democrático*, p. 63.

159. In the coming three years the broad calendar is: Costa Rica – general elections 1996; El Salvador – general elections 1994; Guatemala – general elections originally scheduled for 1995; Honduras – general elections 1993; Nicaragua – partial and municipal elections 1994 and general elections 1996; Panama – general elections 1994.

160. PARLACEN, established under the 1987 Esquipulas accord as a deliberative forum to be based in that town, held its first meeting in late October 1991. Each country was supposed to elect twenty members, but Costa Rica and Nicaragua failed to do so, and revised statutes allow for the body's operation with only three member-states. Despite spirited argument from Sir Henry Plumb, head of the British Conservative Members of the European Parliament, Costa Rican conservative opinion held the regional parliament to be a threat to national sovereignty. CAR, 17 Jan. 1989; 29 Sept. 1989; 5 July 1991; 1 Nov. 1991.

161. The office of Defender of the People was finally established by the Costa Rican Assembly, by a vote of 32 to 15, in April 1993 to guard against general abuses of state power. Ombudsmen charged specifically to deal with human rights matters existed in El Salvador, Guatemala and Honduras. The principal argument of those opposed to the institution of this new office in Costa Rica was that the judicial system already provided sufficient protection for citizens. Ibid., 16 April 1993. At the same time there was a major controversy in San José over the case of the Supreme Court judge, Jesús Ramírez, alleged to have impeded the prosecution of a number of drugs cases and re-appointed on the basis of insufficient contrary votes. Ibid., 26 March 1993.

162. Harold Tyler, 'The Churchwomen's Murders: A Report to the Secretary of State', Washington 1983, p. 4, quoted in Benjamin C. Schwarz, *American Counter-insurgency Doctrine in El Salvador*, Santa Monica 1991, p. 33. CAR, 18 Sept. 1992; Cerdas Cruz et al., *Tarea Inconclusa*, table 26.

163. The sole case to go to court was that of the murder in June 1990 of Michael Devine by soldiers in the Petén. Devine was a US citizen, and Washington publicly demanded the prosecution of a culprit from Cerezo. CAR, 28 Sept. 1990. WOLA, *Political Transition and the Rule of Law in Guatemala*, Washington 1988.

164. CAR, 16 July 1993.

165. *Barricada Internacional*, 5 May 1990.

166. Carlos Vilas, 'Class, Lineage and Politics in Contemporary Nicaragua', *Journal of Latin American Studies*, vol. 24, part 2, May 1992, which provides fascinating detail on the elite and criticizes some of the wilder claims made in Samuel Stone, *The Heritage of the Conquistadors*, Lincoln, Neb. 1990.

167. *El País*, Madrid, 25 April 1990.

168. According to Carlos Fonseca Terán, son of one of the FSLN's founders, those who saw differences within the bourgeoisie and sought an alliance with the Las Palmas group were 'stupid' because that faction aimed

> to eliminate Sandinismo as an ideology, making the Sandinistas bourgeois, prompting them to abandon their class position. Most leading Sandinista cadres, if not the rank and file, have already bitten. It is in the bourgeoisie's interest to preserve the FSLN as a political force – a social democratic one.

El Diario Nuevo, Managua, 28 Aug. 1990, quoted in Patterson and Roulston, 'Sandinistas in Opposition', p. 237.

169. Ibid., p. 236; CAR, 6 April 1990.

170. CAR, 30 March 1990.

171. Ibid., 4 May 1990.

172. Ibid., 13 July 1990.

173. The *Guardian*, 10 July 1990.

174. Patterson and Roulston, 'Sandinistas in Opposition', pp. 232–5.

175. Ibid., p. 246; CAR, 22 Nov. 1991.

176. Quoted in Patterson and Roulston, 'Sandinistas in Opposition', p. 243.

177. Ibid., pp. 242ff.

178. The *Guardian*, 21 Sept. 1992. A State Department official commented that 'Helms is trying to save the country by destroying it'. (*Newsweek*, 14 Sept. 1992.) If lack of concerted and public opposition to this might be expected from the Bush administration, the failure of the Clinton government to oppose it the following year constituted a highly reprehensible piece of cowardice as well as a major error.

179. CAR, 30 Oct. 1992.

180. Ibid., 19 Feb. 1993.

181. Ibid., 30 Oct. 1992; 6 Nov. 1992.

182. Ibid., 6 Nov. 1992.

183. The protocol mentioned no names, and Ortega could readily be replaced by General Cuadra or Colonel Oswaldo Lacayo (Cuadra's cousin and deputy chief of staff), both respected professionals as well as diligent guarantors of the Sandinistas' heritage.

184. The EPS openly sold equipment worth an estimated $17.5 million to Peru and Ecuador. CAR, 30 April 1993.

185. Immediately after the elections there was much talk of changing the EPS's title. By 1993 the high command's needs to develop a more institutionalized, non-partisan image reduced opposition to this, one proposed alternative being the name given by Sandino in 1926 to his guerrilla force: 'Army of the Defence of National Sovereignty'.

186. Quoted in *El País*, 25 Sept. 1993.

187. The conditions included the important provision that Salvadoreans living abroad – a large constituency – be properly enfranchised, and that the rebels' allies Convergencia Democrática (CD) be included in the electoral tribunal. Useful surveys of the FMLN over this period may be found in: Tommie Sue Montgomery, 'Armed Struggle and Popular Resistance in El Salvador: The Struggle for Peace', in Barry Carr and Steve Ellner, eds., *The Latin American Left. From the Fall of Allende to Perestroika*, London 1993; Sara Miles

THE PACIFICATION OF CENTRAL AMERICA

and Bob Ostertag, 'The FMLN: New Thinking', in Anjali Sundaram and George Gelber, eds., *A Decade of War. El Salvador Confronts the Future*, London 1991.

188. Tommie Sue Montgomery identifies six periods: mass struggle, 1970–March 1980; transition, March 1980–Jan. 1981; armed struggle, Jan. 1981–1984; armed and political struggle, 1984–88; negotiating struggle, 1989–91; political struggle by other means, 1992–. *The Latin American Left*, pp. 103–4. This periodization does not exactly correspond to programmatic debates and shifts within the FMLN.

189. Miles and Ostertag, pp. 218–22. The expression of such flexibility at a politically strategic level with the adoption of pragmatism and open reconsideration of the traditions of a Marxist-Leninist programme was most publicly undertaken by Comandante Joaquín Villalobos in an article – 'A Democratic Revolution for El Salvador' – published in the far from radical US journal *Foreign Policy* in the spring of 1989. In a simultaneous interview in Nicaragua, Villalobos synthesized his message for a friendlier audience:

The Salvadorean revolution is taking place in the context not only of a profound capitalist crisis, but also a crisis of socialism . . . This calls into question many of what we might call 'scientific certainties', and opens the road to new kinds of revolutions in which, for example, the idea of societies of single parties is liquidated. We Salvadorean revolutionaries at first were also ideologically rigid, by necessity, in order to survive and develop. But later new conditions were created which offered the opportunity to develop our own thinking.

The FMLN is proposing an open, pluralist project, which will be pragmatically inserted in our domestic and geopolitical reality. What is fundamental is not its ideological definition but whether it resolves El Salvador's problems or not.

Pensamiento Propio, Managua, April 1989, quoted in Miles and Ostertag, pp. 241–2. For Villalobos's appraisal of the political situation following the peace accords, see *Diario Latino*, San Salvador, 14 Jan. 1993.

190. Miles and Ostertag, pp. 218, 240.

191. Montgomery, pp. 113–14; Schwarz, p. 13, fn 24.

192. Montgomery, p. 115. This difference was quite evident at the time, as was the FMLN's adaptation to its failure immediately to seize control of the administrative centre of the capital. For my own reaction at the time, see the *Guardian*, 1 Dec. 1989.

193. Good surveys of the shifting currents within the Salvadorean right may be found in: Chris Norton, 'The Hard Right: ARENA Comes to Power', in Sundaram and Gelber, eds., *A Decade of War*; and Sara Miles and Bob Ostertag, 'D'Aubuissón's New ARENA', *NACLA*, vol. XXIII, no. 2, July 1989. An excellent appraisal of the political situation of El Salvador in the autumn of 1991 is given in J. Tulchin, ed., *Is There a Transition to Democracy in El Salvador?*, Washington 1992.

194. A.J. Bracevich, J. Hallums, R. White and T. Young, *American Military Policy in Small Wars: the Case of El Salvador*, Washington 1988, p. 47.

195. Schwarz, *American Counter-insurgency*, p. 22. The most reliable recent survey of the military is Knut Walter and Philip J. Williams, 'The Military and Democracy in El Salvador', *Journal of Inter-American Studies*, vol. 35, no. 1, 1993.

196. Bracevich et al., p. 9; Congressional Research Service, *El Salvador, 1979–89: A Briefing Book*, Washington 1989, p. 101.

197. Schwarz, *American Counter-insurgency*, pp. 19–21.

198. Ibid., p. 21.

199. The final document with appendices is seventy-eight pages long. *Acuerdos de Chapultepec*, Mexico 1992.

200. A further important provision for the judicial sphere was the considerable limitation placed on the powers of courts martial. For an admirably clear description of the accord's main features and early implementation, see CIIR, *El Salvador. Wager for Peace*, London 1993. An early critical analysis is given in David Holiday and William Stanley, 'Building the Peace: Preliminary Lessons from El Salvador', *Journal of*

International Affairs, vol. 46, no. 2, winter 1993.

201. The Truth Commission's members were Belisario Betancourt (Chair, ex-president of Colombia); Reinaldo Figueredo (ex-foreign minister of Venezuela); and Thomas Berguenthal (professor of international law, George Washington University, USA). The commission had a staff of over seventy, including ten forensic anthropologists and ballistics experts. 'De la Locura a la Esperanza. Informe de la Comisión de la Verdad para El Salvador', *Diario Latino*, 2 April 1993, p. 89.

202. The members of the Ad Hoc Commission were Abraham Rodríguez, a leading Duarte adviser; Eduardo Molina, a PDC founder; Reynaldo Galindo Pohl, a bureaucrat with international experience. This membership was accepted without great protest by right-wing circles. Holiday and Stanley, p. 425.

203. CAR, 18 Aug. 1993. See also note 88. On 5 August 1993 ONUSAL reported that it had destroyed most of the weaponry from forty-one FMLN arsenals revealed in El Salvador, Honduras and Nicaragua. The weaponry destroyed between the accord's deadline of 15 December 1992 and the post-explosion report date imposed by ONUSAL included 10,000 individual guns, 4 million bullets, 9,000 grenades and 139 rockets. ANSA wire, 18 Aug. 1993.

204. CAR, 16 Oct. 1992; 13 Nov. 1992. The crisis of November 1992 resulted in an agreement to allow Cristiani to delay acting on the commission's report until 15 January 1993.

205. A sense of the changed climate in the USA may be gleaned from the title of a *Newsweek* article reporting the amnesty: 'Truth – But No Consequences. If no one gets punished, why expose the crime?' (*Newsweek*, 29 March 1993.) Even *The Economist*, which prides itself on Olympian detachment, registered the strength of opinion as well as the political dilemmas involved. *The Economist*, 20 March 1993. US Secretary of State Warren Christopher responded by setting up an investigation into Washington's involvement in the war. Issued in late July 1993, this report did not directly accuse US personnel of lying but declared that 'there were definitely cases when policy advocacy spilled over into statements that were perceived as misleading Congress or conveying "disinformation"'. Specific instances of wrongdoing in this regard were the El Mozote massacre of 1981 and the execution of the US religious women in 1980. Ibid., 10 Sept. 1993.

206. *Diario Latino*, 2 April 1993, p. 74. All three commanders belonged to the ERP, and Villalobos and Martínez were FMLN negotiators. The Truth Commission's remit covered the period 1980 to 1991, but if it had been extended back to 1975 Villalobos would have had to explain his role in the execution of his comrade Roque Dalton – a killing that still resonated strongly within the Salvadorean left nearly twenty years later. For a remarkable interview with Villalobos by Dalton's son, Juan José, see *Presencia*, 30 May 1993, which might usefully be read in tandem with Villalobos's current celebration of pluralism.

207. Holiday and Stanley, p. 424.

208. CIIR, *Wager for Peace*, pp. 18–19; CAR, 7 May 1993.

209. See, for example, CAR, 11 Aug. 1989.

210. On the right there was intermittent but perceptible recourse to violent settlement of internal disputes – not, perhaps, unnatural, given the dependency of this sector on the death squads. The first probable case was the killing of ARENA leader and Cristiani's first minister of presidency José Antonio Rodríguez Porth. On the left there was a strong suspicion that the 23 May 1993 explosion in Managua of the cache run by the FMLN was the work of their 'allies' in the ERP, reflecting a long-standing feud between the two organizations.

211. Early in September 1993 the FMLN resolved – after quite fierce debate – to support the 1994 presidential candidacy of CD leader Rubén Zamora, nominating as his vice-presidential partner Francisco Lima, a prominent businessman and briefly vice-president in 1967 for the conservative PCN before founding the UDN, subsequently used by the Communist Party as a legal front.

212. For a broader and deeper discussion of the Guatemalan case in a comparative

context, see Gabriel Aguilera, 'Esquipulas y el Conflicto Interno en Centroamérica', in Ricardo Córdova and Raul Benítez, eds., *La Paz en Centroamérica. Expediente de Documentos Fundamentales*, Mexico 1989; José Guillermo Monroy Peralta, *Desafíos para la Paz en Guatemala. De la Guerra a la Negociación Política, 1960–1991*, PhD thesis, UNAM, Mexico 1992.

213. Quoted in CAR, 22 Nov. 1991.

214. For the repression of the 1980s, see Carmack, *Harvest of Violence*; Susanne Jonas, *The Battle for Guatemala*, Boulder 1991; Jean-Marie Simon, *Guatemala: Eternal Spring, Eternal Tyranny*, New York 1987.

215. CEPAL, *Impacto de las Migraciones*, p. 20; CIIR, *Guatemala. Transition from Terror?*, London 1993; Liz Oglesby, 'Return and Reintegration of Guatemala's Refugees and Internally Displaced Populations. A Presentation of the Research of Myrna Mack', Columbia University, conference paper no. 53, New York 1991.

216. Comité pro Justicia y Paz de Guatemala, 'The Guatemalan Civil Defence Patrols', London 1990; CAR, 18 May 1990; Monroy, *Paz en Centroamérica*, p. 77.

217. Richard Wilson, 'Anchored Communities', p. 132; 'Machine Guns and Mountain Spirits'.

218. The best contemporaneous analysis of Cerezo and the DCG is James Painter, *Guatemala. False Hope. False Freedom*, 2nd ed., London 1989.

219. Quoted in Monroy, *Paz en Guatemala*, p. 128.

220. For general discussion, see Jonas, *Battle for Guatemala*; Painter, *False Hope*. For analysis of the state of play in 1993, CAR, 2 April 1993; 9 July 1993.

221. The agenda agreed was: (1) democratization and human rights; (2) strengthening of civil institutions and the role of the military in a democratic society; (3) identity and rights of the indigenous peoples; (4) constitutional reforms and electoral organization; (5) socio-economic matters; (6) agrarian situation; (7) resettlement of displaced people; (8) re-incorporation of URNG into political life; (9) arrangements for a definitive ceasefire; (10) timetable for implementation and verification of accords; (11) signature of firm and lasting peace, and demobilization.

222. CAR, 19 June 1992. On 8 July 1993 de León Carpio presented a new peace plan, developed by Héctor Rosada Granada, which projected the parallel negotiation of broad issues important to the URNG and a narrow strand related to obtaining a ceasefire and demobilization, the only issue that the army was really prepared to take seriously. Several days before the proposal the members of the CNR resigned in order to give the new government a free hand. Ibid., 16 July 1993.

223. Apart from their alleged links with the drug trade, the Cerezo family was being investigated for irregular sale of passports and purchase of helicopters. Ibid., 30 March 1990; 9 Oct. 1992.

224. Ibid., 26 March 1993; 18 June 1993.

225. Ibid., 11 Sept. 1992.

226. Ibid., 9 Oct. 1992; 29 Jan. 1993.

227. Ibid., 2 July 1993.

228. There is a sharp need for case studies on the Guatemalan electricity industry – particularly the construction and management of the Chixoy hydroelectric project, which provides 65 per cent of national supply – and the capital's transport system. The daily subsidy rate is my own calculation, based on the government's agreement in 1990 to pay Q0.095 per pass for the 1.4 million rides provided by the 1,154 buses then operating. Ibid., 18 May 1990; 25 May 1990. For the issue of oil subsidies and consumption, see ibid., 30 Nov. 1990; 5 July 1991. The crisis of late May 1990 clearly relates in its causes to that of almost exactly three years later which had far greater political impact because, in my view, of the intervening decay of any vestigial popular expectations of civilian government short of a comprehensive peace settlement.

229. Ibid., 9 July 1993.

230. Piero Gleijeses, *Shattered Hope. The Guatemalan Revolution and the United States, 1944–1954*, Princeton 1991.

Appendices

Appendix 1   Select Political Chronology, 1987–93

1987		*Country*	
Jan.		CR	Pres. Arias announces peace plan focused on ending Contra campaign in return for FSLN concessions over internal Nicaraguan regime.
Feb.		CR	Arias calls presidential summit, excluding Daniel Ortega, to discuss his plan; Ortega initially calls CR a 'neocolony' but later (18th) accepts plan's outline; others express shock at anti-Contra provisions.
May	18	Nica	four killed in Contra attack on rural co-op.
	23	Guate	initiation of URNG radio station La Voz Popular.
June	1	El S	Pres. Duarte rejects FMLN proposals for talks.
	5	Guate	third anniversary of Grupo de Apoyo Mutuo (GAM).
	6	Pa	Gen. John Galvin replaced by Gen. Fred Woerner as head of US Southern Command (SouthCom).
	7	Pa	Col. Roberto Díaz Herrera, second-in-command of Defence Forces (FDP), removed from office; accuses Gen. Noriega of rigging 1984 poll and ordering murder of Dr Hugo Spadafora.
	9	El S	FMLN temporarily occupy Jiquilisco.
		Pa	establishment of business-led National Civic Crusade (CCN) opposition movement.
	11	El S	Duarte talks with Philip Habib, US special envoy for Central America.
	12	El S	Duarte cancels regional meeting due on 25th over Arias plan.
	17	USA	Reagan tells Arias his plan is too lenient towards Nicaragua.
	25	CR	Foreign Minister Rodrigo Madrigal requests US explanation for training of Contras on Costa Rican territory.
	27	CR	Arias tours region to lobby for his plan.
	28	El S	government–FMLN agreement for evacuation of ninety-eight wounded rebels.
	29	Pa	commercial and school strikes called by CCN against Noriega.
July	1	Pa	OAS passes resolution calling on US to cease interference in internal Panamanian affairs, as guaranteed under 1977 treaties.
	2	Guate	reports of meeting in Mexico between Pres. Cerezo and URNG; Cerezo declares guerrilla surrender is prerequisite to talks.
	9	El S	fifteen demonstrating social security workers wounded by police.

27	Pa	Col. Díaz arrested after assault on his house; formally retracts allegations against Noriega.
29	Guate	UNHCR appoints Hector Gross special rapporteur.
	Hon	under Mexican pressure, Honduran government withdraws 'spoiling' draft amendment to peace plan at presidential summit in Tegucigalpa; agreement that ceasefires to be between governments and rebels and that all external aid to rebels should be halted.

Aug. 5	Guate	82-year-old Gonzalo Menéndez de la Riva appointed human rights ombudsman, without power to bring cases to court; Cerezo meets GAM.
	USA	Reagan and Speaker Jim Wright issue peace plan to pre-empt regional proposal.
7	Region	Central American presidents sign peace accord at Esquipulas, Guatemala.
8	Hon	six US soldiers injured by bomb, Comayagua.
	Pa	US aid suspended.
28	El S	political prisoners attacked in Mariona prison.
31	Pa	anti-Noriega strike movement fizzles out.

Sept. 3	El S	end of three-month strike by 15,000 social security employees.
4	El S	FMLN attack coffee-processing plants.
13	Nica	return of Monseñor Bismark Caballo and other pro-Contra priests.
16	Guate	National Assembly approves new tax law, attacked by business front CACIF.
21	Nica	*La Prensa* permitted to resume publication; government promises to re-open Radio Católica, closed in Jan. 1986.

Oct. 1	Nica	government declares unilateral ceasefire in provinces of Jinotega, Nueva Segovia and Zelaya until 7 Nov. deadline set at Esquipulas; Contras reject this.
4	El S	government–FMLN talks at papal nunciature.
5	Nica	Contra commander Uriel Vanegas and 100 troops sign peace treaty.
9	Guate	first official government–URNG talks end in Madrid after two days.
10	Guate	government withdraws tax reforms after CACIF strike threat.
13	CR	Oscar Arias awarded Nobel Peace Prize.
23	El S	Rubén Zamora and Guillermo Ungo (FDR) return after seven years.
29	El S	FDR–FMLN withdraw from talks after murder of human rights leader Herbert Anaya.

Nov. 3	El S	FMLN starts three-day traffic stoppage.
5	El S	Duarte amnesties 400 political prisoners and declares fifteen-day ceasefire.

	11	El S	airforce breaks ceasefire, bombing Los Dubones, Chalatcnango.
	15	El S	all political parties except governing PDC withdraw from National Reconciliation Commission established under terms of Esquipulas.
	29	El S	Zamora (MPSC) and Ungo (MNR) join Social Democratic Party (PSD) to form Convergencia Democrática (CD), expressing tactical differences with FMLN.
Dec.	30	Guate	leaders of eleven peasant movements form Confederación Nacional Campesina (CNC) to press for land reform.

1988

Jan	13	Guate	15,000 march in capital against electricity price rises.
	16	Region	presidential summit at Alajuela, Costa Rica, includes Nicaragua whilst Reagan requests US Congress to approve $270 million for Contras.
	21	Region	at Alajuela, Ortega accepts requirement of Arias plan to talk directly with Contras; Reagan reduces Contra aid request to $36 million.
Feb.	3	USA	Congress votes against Contra aid.
	4	Pa	US grand jury indicts Noriega on narcotics and racketeering charges.
	10	Pa	José Blandón, former consul in New York, makes detailed testimony against Noriega to US Senate sub-committee.
	14	Nica	severe deflationary programme introduced; direct government–Contra talks start in Guatemala.
	26	Pa	after talks with US ambassador, Pres. Eric Delvalle tries to remove Noriega as FDP commander and is himself promptly deposed by National Assembly; Manuel Solís Palma appointed in his stead, but USA continues to recognize Delvalle as legal head of state.
Mar.	6	Nica	army opens dry-season offensive against Contras.
	11	Pa	US withholds payments to Canal Commission.
	16	Pa	news of abortive police coup provokes anti-Noriega riots and two-week general strike; FDP purged.
	19	Pa	state of emergency declared; banks closed (for nine weeks); 'Dignity Battalions' formed by Noriega, who holds secret talks with US envoys.
	20	El S	elections: ARENA wins effective control of National Assembly and nearly three-quarters of municipalities.
		Pa	US Secretary of State Shultz publicly urges Noriega to go into exile in Spain.

	22	Pa	Noriega offers to resign but insists on choosing his own time.
	23	Nica	agreement at Sapoá for sixty-day ceasefire from 1 April to allow talks and relocation of Contra troops into designated zones.
Apr.	1	Pa	anti-Noriega strikes fizzle out.
	2	El S	ARENA claims electoral fraud deprives it of clear control of Assembly.
	5	Pa	1,300 US troops sent to bolster 10,000 already in Canal Zone.
	7	Hon	riots follow extradition of citizen to USA for narcotics offences; US consulate burnt and four protestors killed by guards.
	8	Pa	Reagan uses 1977 Emergency Powers Act to install economic boycott.
	17	Nica	Contras reject government proposal for permanent ceasefire; private talks between government and Contra leader Alfredo César.
	18	Guate	CUC leadership (including Rigoberta Menchú) return for week-long visit; temporarily arrested.
	24	Guate	local elections: DCG win over half of 271 municipalities; seven-party right-wing alliance wins only 34.
		Pa	Solís appoints leftist cabinet; Church calls for lifting of US sanctions.
	26	Guate	junior officers in highlands combat zones accuse high command of drug-smuggling and profiteering.
	27	Pa	US disowns plans to remove Noriega and suggests compromise.
May	1	El S	military helicopters drop propaganda on 20,000-strong march, which passes without violence.
	9	Pa	banks re-open; US Assistant Secretary of State Michael Kozak holds talks with Noriega offering to drop charges if he leaves country.
	10	Nica	Comandante 'Fernando', leader of mutiny against Contra military chief Enrique Bermúdez, detained by Honduran army.
	11	Guate	abortive coup attempt in garrisons of Jutiapa and Retalhuleu.
	14	El S	PDC leaders Julio Rey Prendes and Fidel Chávez Mena hold separate conventions.
	15	Hon	ambassador to Panama, Col. Rigoberto Regalado, arrested at Miami airport with 11kg of cocaine in bags.
	26	El S	ARENA secures majority in new Assembly.
		Nica	at Managua talks with Contra leadership government drops insistence on negotiating political questions exclusively with legal opposition; César retreats from agreement.

June	9	Nica	fifth round of talks fail when César introduces new demands (right of conscripts to leave ranks at any time; return of all confiscated property; removal of Supreme Court judges); government reveals existence of talks with César.
	14	Guate	closure of weekly *La Epoca* after offices bombed.
		Nica	price and wages controls lifted.
	22	Guate	Congress declares amnesty for perpetrators of political crimes.
	23	El S	PDC leadership backs Chávez Mena's candidacy.
July	10	Nica	police break up opposition rally at Nandaime and arrest thirty-eight.
	11	Nica	US Ambassador Richard Melton and seven of his staff expelled for 'orchestrating destabilization'.
	12	USA	twelve Nicaraguan diplomats expelled.
	16	Nica	election of Enrique Bermúdez to civilian Contra leadership threatens schism in movement.
	19	Nica	government extends ceasefire to 30 August.
	27	Pa	Reagan announces that covert destabilization of Noriega regime has been authorized.
	30	Guate	three civilian rightists arrested for plotting coup.
Aug.	9	Nica	US Congress approves $27 million 'humanitarian' aid to Contras, and rejects payment of $16.5 million military aid frozen since 1986.
	13	El S	1,300 refugees return from Mesa Grande camp in Honduras.
	21	El S	ten unarmed peasants killed by army in San Francisco; Duarte promises investigation.
	22	Guate	major strike against price rises.
	23	Guate	URNG meets National Reconciliation Commission, which lacks powers to negotiate, in Costa Rica.
	31	El S	according to FECMAFAM (mothers of disappeared and political prisoners), 139 people have disappeared since Esquipulas Accord.
Sept.	11	El S	Julio Rey Prendes formalizes split in PDC by forming MADC.
		Guate	attack on Father Andrés Girón, leader of agrarian reform movement.
	12	Guate	first public appearance of CONAVIGUA widows' association.
	13	El S	FMLN successfully attacks El Paraiso HQ of 4th Infantry Batallion.
	15	Pa	Miami judge restricts information on charges against Noriega during US election campaign.
	19	El S	capital paralysed by forty-eight-hour FMLN public transport boycott.
	30	Nica	government unilaterally extends ceasefire for fifth time.

Oct.	4	Hon	government requests UN to provide peace-keeping force for border.
	6	Chile	Gen. Pinochet loses plebiscite; poll now to be held in Dec. 1989.
	8	Guate	agreement with UK and Belize to drafting of treaty recognizing Belizean independence.
	13	USA	government desists from further efforts to gain aid for Contra whilst Reagan in office.
	22	Region	Hurricane Joan hits Nicaraguan coast, killing 116 and leaving 200,000 homeless; El Salvador less severely affected.
	25	El S	FMLN leaders Joaquín Villalobos and Leonel González make first diplomatic appearance meeting Pres. Arias in Costa Rica.
	31	El S	Chief of Staff Gen. Adolfo Blandón replaced by Col. René Emilio Ponce, CO 3rd Brigade and graduate of 1966 ('*tandona*') class.
Nov.	2	El S	government rejects FMLN talks offer; FMLN attacks National Police HQ.
		Nica	currency devalued by 72 per cent.
	8	USA	Vice-President George Bush wins presidential election.
	14–19	Region	OAS meeting in San Salvador; Secretary of State Shultz criticizes lack of support for US measures against Managua.
	15	El S	50,000-strong march demands peace negotiations.
	24	Guate	twenty-two people killed by army at El Aguacate, Chimaltenango; according to Americas Watch state forces responsible for 621 killings in 1988.
	27	Nica	sixth devaluation (by 72 per cent) of new Córdoba, introduced in Feb.
Dec.	3	Hon	end of successful ten-day SITRATERCO strike against United Brands over company recognition of parallel unions.
	4	Hon	primary elections: Rafael Leonardo Callejas wins PN nomination; Carlos Flores leads PL field of four.
	7	Guate	according to *Prensa Libre*, thirty nine people killed and twelve disappeared between 27 Nov. and 3 Dec.
		Hon	Pres. Azcona demands departure of Contras from national territory.

1989

Jan.	1	Cuba	thirtieth anniversary of the Revolution.
		El S	according to the Church, 1,369 soldiers, rebels and civilians killed in 1988.
	2	Guate	over seventy killed when ferry capsizes off Caribbean coast.
	3	Nica	Vice-Pres. Ramírez rules out further talks with Contra.

3	Pa	encouraged by US, opposition decides to contest May poll.
13	El S	government admits that fifty-two mayors have resigned following FMLN threats.
20	El S	FMLN mortars Policía de Hacienda HQ.
	Guate	Cerezo rejects URNG offer of talks in Caracas.
23	El S	FMLN offers to participate in elections if postponed until Sept.
25	Hon	assassination of former army chief Gen. Alvarez Martínez.

Feb. 1	Nica	new austerity measures aim to reduce public spending by half, ending foodstuff subsidies and reducing army by 25,000.
	El S	FMLN suspends action against non-military US personnel after 'positive reaction' by Washington to its proposals.
2	Region	presidents (except ailing Duarte) meet at Caracas for inauguration of Carlos Andrés Pérez; Ortega agrees to open elections with international observers; others promise diplomatic pressure on Contras.
	Para-guay	thirty-four-year dictatorship of Gen. Stroessner overthrown in coup.
3	El S	visiting US Vice-Pres. Quayle warns military to improve human rights record.
13	El S	Defence Minister Vides Casanova warns of military coup if poll delayed.
15	Region	five presidents meet at Tesoro Beach, El Salvador; agree to demobilize Contras in Honduras; Nicaragua agrees to reform constitution and advance elections to Feb. 1990.
17	El S	PDC convenes meeting of parties to discuss FMLN offers.
21	Nica	government talks with opposition parties on poll arrangements.
24	Nica	US Vice-Pres. Quayle sharpens Bush's criticism (16th) of Tesoro Beach accords and re-affirms support for Contra.

Mar. 8	Guate	forty-fifth session of UNHCR condemns human rights abuses but desists from sending special rapporteur.
10	El S	10,000-strong march supports FMLN demand for poll delay.
14	Hon	after visit by US Under-Secretary of State Robert Kimmit, government supports humanitarian aid for Contra whilst redeployment underway.
17	Nica	1,900 ex-members of National Guard released and ten expelled priests admitted under Esquipulas accords.
19	El S	elections: ARENA's Alfredo Cristiani wins 53.8 per cent of presidential vote.

113

24	USA	Pres. Bush announces agreement with Congress to provide Contra with $41 million 'humanitarian' aid until Feb. 1990; US requests Honduras to leave Contra unmolested until then.
30	Guate	end of four-day uprising and siege at El Pavón prison; ten dead and sixty wounded.

Apr. 3	Cuba	visit by Soviet leader Gorbachev amidst rumours of rift between Havana and Moscow.
	Guate	Amoco ends three years of oil exploration in Huehuetenango and El Quiché on grounds of EGP harassment.
8	El S	Pres.-elect Cristiani, in USA, rejects FMLN demands for fresh poll as condition for talks.
13	Nica	US Congress formally approves $49.8 million of 'non-lethal' aid to Contras for period up to Feb. 1990 after new Secretary of State James Baker arranges controversial bipartisan accord to keep the Nicaraguan rebels 'armed but inactive'.
18	Nica	electoral law reformed to enfranchise those who boycotted 1984 poll; surprised congressional opposition walks out claiming insufficient guarantees; US and regional governments openly doubt Sandinista goodwill.

May 3	Nica	Pres. Ortega accuses Pres. Arias of 'flagrant violation' of Esquipulas accords at February Tesoro Beach meeting.
4	USA	Oliver North found guilty of charges of deceiving Congress, shredding evidence and taking a bribe.
6	UK	Thatcher rebukes Ortega for failing to introduce 'genuine democracy'.
7	Pa	elections: widespread allegations of fraud to deny victory of opposition ADOC candidate Guillermo Endara.
9	Guate	Defence Minister Gen. Gramajo suppresses coup attempt by retired officers backed by airforce units.
11	Pa	US dispatches extra 2,000 troops and armour to Canal Zone.
17	Pa	OAS foreign ministers condemn poll-rigging and send investigative mission; opposition protest strike rapidly collapses.
18	Pa	OAS formally condemns electoral fraud and attempts to negotiate.

June 1	El S	inauguration of Cristiani amidst widespread power-cuts by FMLN; Gen. Humberto Larios named defence minister after conflict in ARENA.
3	China	massacre of pro-democracy students in Tiananmen Square.
4	Nica	foundation of opposition front, UNO, which immediately exhibits divisions.

	4	Poland	elections: Solidarity wins 99 of 100 parliamentary seats it is permitted to contest.
	9	El S	assassination of José Antonio Rodríguez Porth, minister to the presidency; FMLN denies responsibility.
	12	Nica	'Black Monday': 100 per cent devaluation; fuel prices doubled and those of food rise by up to 80 per cent; new electoral tribunal appointed in which FSLN surrenders the majority permitted by its 1984 poll result.
	14	USA	Senate confirms Bernard Aronson as assistant secretary of state for inter-American affairs, a post vacant since the resignation of Eliott Abrams in January.
	19	Guate	Commission for Human Rights reports 197 extra-judicial killings and forty-one disappearances between January and April 1989.
	22	Guate	US House of Representatives approves $9 million military aid on condition that human rights abuses are investigated.
	23	El S	government introduces severe anti-terrorist measures into penal code.
July	5	Hon	security police (FUSEP) kill cement workers' leader José Danilo Martínez.
	7	Pa	200 protesters block entrance to US Fort Clayton infantry base.
	8	Pa	US tanks and helicopters manoeuvre around Noriega's office at Fort Amador.
	11	Guate	50,000 rally in support of teachers' strike.
	13	Guate	teachers' supporters paralyse centre of capital; subsequent eighteen-day hunger strike obtains meeting with Cerezo.
		Cuba	execution of Gen. Arnaldo Ochoa and others for drug-smuggling.
	14	Nica	Ortega agrees in San José to open dialogue with combined opposition.
	21	El S	US House of Representatives approves $433 million economic and $85 million military aid.
	28	El S	Supreme Court declares unconstitutional the January 1980 decree nationalizing coffee export industry.
		Nica	Washington stages strong public lobby of regional governments to oppose further Contra demobilization at forthcoming Tela summit.
Aug.	4	Nica	on eve of regional summit Ortega holds remarkable twenty-two-hour televised meeting with twenty opposition parties, which agree to participate in Feb. 1990 poll.
	5–7	Region	presidential summit at Tela, Honduras, agrees disbanding of Contras by 5 Dec. and calls on OAS and UN to form an International Commission of Support and Verification (CIAV); despite its opposition to

			Contra demobilization the Bush administration offers formal support for agreement and openly criticizes only the deadline; Nicaragua drops its case against Honduras over the Contras in the World Court.
	13	Guate	DCG selects Alfonso Cabrera as 1990 presidential candidate despite bitter opposition from René de León Schlotter.
	15	Guate	GAM offices destroyed by bomb.
	16	Pa	extensive US military manoeuvres.
	21	Guate	three-month teachers' strike ends without pay rise but with back-pay awarded and charges against activists dropped.
	24	Poland	Solidarity forms government.
	31	Pa	Council of State dissolves National Assembly and names provisional government headed by former Attorney General Francisco Rodríguez; OAS mediation abandoned.
Sept.	4	Belize	People's United Party, led by George Price, wins 13 of 15 seats in poll.
	9	Guate	bombs in central Guatemala City prompt US to issue 'advisory warning' to tourists.
	10	El S	FMLN declares ten-day ceasefire from 13th as goodwill gesture over negotiations.
		Germany	10,000 leave GDR through Hungary for West in seventy-two hours.
	15	El S	FMLN–government talks in Mexico City end without result.
	18	Guate	UN delegate Peter Kooijmans declares human rights position 'very serious and worrying'.
	20	El S	US Senate votes $90 million in military aid without conditions over talks or human rights.
	24	Hon	nine wounded by FUSEP in land occupation, San Pedro Sula.
	26	El S	FMLN launch post-truce attacks in ten out of fourteen provinces.
Oct.	2	Pa	Gen. Maxwell Thurman takes command of US SouthCom.
	3	Pa	abortive coup attempt by Major Moisés Giroldi (later shot); US forces offer only limited support for rebels.
		Nica	visit by Soviet Foreign Minister Shevardnadze, who proposes end of Moscow's military aid in return for halt to Contra activity.
	7	El S	forty-six wounded rebels leave for Cuba after a month's asylum in the capital's cathedral.
	16	El S	second round of talks in San José produces little progress.
	17	Nica	US Senate approves $9 million for the National Endowment for Democracy (established 1983) in order

to finance UNO, now united under candidacy of Violeta Chamorro.

20	Hungary	multi-party politics legalized.
21	Nica	Contras kill eighteen reservists; Ortega cancels unilateral ceasefire; US Senate votes 95–0 to condemn this and fails to implement legal provisions suspending Contra aid in event of aggression.
31	El S	large bomb destroys office of FENASTRAS union, killing nine and wounding forty.

Nov. 1 Nica Ortega ends eighteen-month ceasefire and calls for UN arbitration.

2	El S	FMLN suspends participation in talks, accusing army of responsibility for FENASTRAS bomb.
	Guate	kidnap, rape and torture of US Ursuline nun Diana Ortiz by police.
6	Guate	quetzal deregulated; floats to 3.10 to dollar; sharp rises in price of beans and bread.
8	Region	UN Security Council votes unanimously to deploy 625-strong ONUCA peace-keeping force staffed by Canada, W. Germany and Spain.
9	Germany	Berlin Wall 'falls'.
11	El S	FMLN launches largest offensive since 1981 in San Salvador, occupying thirty *barrios* and attacking presidential palace and residence.
12	El S	state of siege declared; fighting in seven urban centres outside capital; Colapa international airport closed; some 200 killed.
14	El S	FMLN seizes large part of San Miguel; US Secretary of State Baker warns USSR that its support for Central American revolution is biggest obstacle to superpower detente.
15	El S	airforce strafes poor neighbourhoods of San Salvador and San Miguel with high loss of life; execution of Ignacio Ellacuría, rector of University of Central America (UCA), five other Jesuit priests, their housekeeper and her daughter by government troops.
21	El S	FMLN moves into wealthy *barrios* of capital and traps twelve US 'Green Beret' experts in Sheraton Hotel; US House of Representatives votes 215–194 against making portions of 1990 $85 million military aid conditional on investigation of UCA killings.
22	Nica	peace talks broken off when Contras refuse to withdraw 2,000 troops recently deployed.
23	El S	FBI interrogate Lucía Barrera, witness to UCA killings, in Miami and openly disparage her implication of state forces in the crime.
24	El S	National Assembly formally approves comprehensive anti-terrorism law that outlaws virtually every manifestation of public dissent.

26	Hon	election won by National Party candidate Rafael Leonardo Callejas.
	El S	SAM-7 anti-aircraft missiles found in crashed Cessna aircraft in Usulután; diplomatic relations with Nicaragua broken; FMLN completes withdrawal from capital.
30	El S	US repatriates 282 citizens; FMLN declares unilateral ceasefire to facilitate the evacuation.
Dec. 1	Guate	new US Ambassador Thomas Stoock attacks human rights abuses and openly accuses Cerezo acquaintance Col. Hugo Morán of narcotics offences.
	Nica	government prohibits official US team from observing Feb. 1990 poll, but those of UN, OAS and the Jimmy Carter Institute permitted.
3	Guate	Cerezo accuses Salvadorean ARENA of complicity in 9 May coup attempt.
5	Nica	Contra demobilization deadline agreed at Tela summit in August passes without progress.
7	Guate	Ramiro de León Carpio named human rights ombudsman.
10	Nica	one killed and thirty injured at UNO meeting in Masatepe.
	Czecho	establishment of government with non-Communist majority.
10-12	Region	presidential summit at San Isidro de Coronado, Costa Rica, calls for demobilization of guerrillas in both Nicaragua and El Salvador as demanded by Cristiani as condition for attendance; Ortega criticized by FMLN and left abroad for this; presidents also insist that all Contra aid be handed to CIAV.
14	Chile	elections won by Patricio Aylwin and seventeen-party opposition *concertación* alliance led by Christian Democrats.
15	Pa	National Assembly declares war on USA and names Noriega 'maximum leader of the struggle for national liberation'.
20	Pa	24,000 US troops invade in 'Operation Just Cause'; resistance is short-lived; Endara sworn in as president on US military base; opposition estimates 1,000 civilian casualties.
22	Pa	OAS formally censures US invasion as breaking international law.
	Romania	Ceausescu overthrown.
24	Pa	Noriega seeks asylum in papal nunciature.

1990

Jan. 1	Nica	two nuns, one a US citizen, executed by Contras.

	3	Pa	Noriega, exhausted by highly sophisticated heavy-metal sonic barrage, surrenders to US forces.
	7	Guate	URNG claim to have caused 2,370 army casualties in 1,680 actions in 1989.
	12	Guate	assassination of Hector Oqueli, leading figure in Salvadorean FDR, and Guatemalan lawyer Hilda Flores.
	19	El S	nine military personnel formally charged with UCA killings.
		USA	regional tour by Vice-Pres. Quayle radically reduced by Latin American protests at invasion of Panama.
	24	El S	US Assistant Secretary of State Aronson publicly backs talks with FMLN.
	31	El S	Cristiani flies to USA to lobby Congress.
Feb.	5	CR	presidential elections won by Rafael Angel Calderón Fournier (PUSC).
		El S	US Senators Edward Kennedy and John Kerry introduce bill to halt military aid.
	7	Nica	UN commends impartiality of Supreme Electoral Tribunal.
	8	El S	Gen. Maxwell Thurman, CO US SouthCom, tells US Senate Armed Services Committee that the FMLN cannot be beaten.
	10	Nica	government releases 1,000 accused of Contra activities and thirty-nine ex-National Guard officers.
	12	S. Africa	Nelson Mandela released.
	23	El S	José Napoleón Duarte dies of cancer, aged sixty-four.
	25	Nica	Violeta Chamorro (UNO) wins elections with 54.9 per cent of the vote; UNO wins 51 of National Assembly's 93 seats; FSLN takes 39.
Mar.	5	Guate	temporary withdrawal of US Ambassador Stoock in protest at failure to prosecute human rights violations, especially those against US citizens.
	13	Guate	Lt. José Fernando Minera Navas, held on drugs charges, accuses president's brothers of involvement.
		Pa	Endara ends thirteen-day hunger strike in cathedral protesting delay in US aid.
	14	Hon	Callejas government austerity measures include devaluation, dismissal of 2,000 public employees and proposed privatizations.
	20	Guate	Bishop of San Marcos declares that seventy peasants have disappeared in the province since June 1989.
		Nica	outgoing FSLN government passes laws legalizing property confiscations since 1979, protecting minimum wage and university autonomy.
	21	El S	occupation of El Rosario church, San Salvador, in protest at sacking of 11,000 public employees accused of supporting FMLN's November offensive.

23	Guate	ex-president Ríos Montt proclaimed candidate for Frente Republicano Guatemalteco.
25	Nica	Contra agreement with UNO to disarm and occupy security zones by 15 April.
	El S	establishment of Ciudad Segundo Montes by returned refugees in Morazán.
27	Guate	CNR and URNG open talks in Oslo.
	Cuba	US begins transmission of counter-revolutionary TV Martí.

Apr. 4	El S	UN Secretary General Pérez de Cuellar and FMLN agree basis for negotiations in Geneva.
19	Guate	Defence Minister Gramajo receives military delegation demanding new economic policy.
	Nica	new ceasefire; Contras to disarm by 10 June; Humberto Ortega to remain army commander.
	Hon	independent banana growers (CAGSA) sign favourable sales agreement with UK firms provoking conflict with United Brands, which claims exclusive contract still in force.
25	Nica	Chamorro government installed.
26	El S	US House Foreign Relations Committee votes 50 per cent cut in military aid, to be restored only if FMLN fails to negotiate.
	Nica	Vice-Pres. Virgilio Godoy declares UNO split over Chamorro's immediate overtures to defeated FSLN; Contras repudiate agreement of 19th.

May 1	El S	large union demonstrations; fierce FMLN attacks in elite zones.
	Guate	capital and much of Escuintla, Chimaltenango and Sacatepéquez blacked out by URNG pylon attacks.
	USA	Senate approves aid of $420 million for Panama and $300 million for Nicaragua, restoring sugar quotas cut in 1988 and 1984.
6	Nica	new government–Contra pact confirms 10 June deadline for disarming.
13	Hon	sabotage of CAGSA banana shipments, allegedly by pro-United Brands forces.
15	Guate	eighteen of capital's twenty bus companies halt service, demanding 100 per cent price rise.
16	Guate	school students demonstrate against bus companies, are fired on; many schools closed.
17	Nica	Chamorro concedes demands of striking civil servants and sacks labour minister.
18	Guate	Vice-Pres. Roberto Carpio refuses to allow state intervention in bus crisis.
20	Guate	replacement of Gen. Gramajo as defence minister.
21	El S	talks in Caracas mediated by UN's Alvaro de Soto agree broad agenda and calendar for negotiations.

	22	Guate	Cerezo orders army to provide transport assistance in capital.
	26	El S	Cristiani confirms theft of log book central to investigation of UCA killings.
		Guate	government–company talks over bus crisis collapse; Cerezo orders seizure of vehicles, but only twelve of hundreds named are arrested.
	28	Guate	URNG talks with nine political parties in Spain following Oslo accord in March.
	30	Guate	bus service resumed at old fares; students attack several vehicles.
June	1	Guate	URNG renounces sabotage of November elections.
	7	Guate	US House Appropriations Committee reduces military aid by 70 per cent owing to human rights abuses.
	8	CR	death of ex-President José Figueres.
		Guate	US citizen Michael Devine killed at Poptún, El Petén.
	9	Hon	'Banana War' ends with help of EC mediation.
	15	Nica	government announces plan to cut army by 50 per cent by 3 Aug.
	17	Region	summit in Antigua promotes regional trade plan.
	19	El S	six days of talks at Oaxtepec; FMLN insists on structural changes in armed forces.
	21	El S	US Congress votes aid of $15.7 million for military in 1991, 50 per cent to be cut if talks halt or no progress made on UCA case.
	27	Nica	surrender of 100 Contra leaders, including Israel Galeano.
	29	Hon	strike on United Brands banana plantation.
		Nica	8,000 public employees strike for pay rise and against decrees returning property confiscated under FSLN rule.
July	8	Cuba	USSR announces economic aid to be phased out.
	13	Nica	government offers public sector workers 43 per cent rise and withdrawal of decrees privatizing state farms after eleven-day general strike and riots.
	17	El S	five days of talks in Costa Rica; FMLN calls for replacement of armed forces high command.
	20	El S	talks halt with deadlock on military question, now at the core of negotiations.
	24	CR	twenty-four-hour strike by 170,000 public employees protesting austerity measures.
	26	El S	agreement for UN commission (ONUSAL) to monitor human rights abuses.
		Hon	Pres. Callejas offers to mediate between FESINTRANH and United Brands.
Aug.	2	Guate	URNG announces sabotage campaign to be resumed because of renewed army repression.
		Kuwait	invasion by Iraq.

6	Hon	forty-three-day banana strike ends after military intervention.
8	Nica	removal of airforce commander Col. Javier Pichardo Ramírez, alleged to be favourable to a leftist coup.
13	Nica	Chamorro pardons four men serving thirty-year sentences for murdering her husband in 1978.
15	Hon	twelve alleged Cinchonero guerrillas killed in abortive bank raid at El Zamorano.
16	Nica	return of Luis Somoza, nephew of dictator Anastasio, to reclaim family land and revive the Liberal Party.
22	El S	talks in Costa Rica collapse over military question after four days.
25	Guate	500 police participate in DEA raid on poppy fields, San Marcos.
29	Guate	Ríos Montt's candidacy ruled unconstitutional by Supreme Election Board because he previously led a de facto regime.
Sept. 3	El S	Judge Ricardo Zamora orders arrest of four members of Atlacatl Battalion accused of perjury in UCA case.
	Guate	troops surround house of Gen. Juan José Marroquín, who is replaced as chief of staff.
11	Guate	assassination of sociologist Myrna Mack.
12	Guate	Supreme Court orders Election Board to restore Ríos Montt's candidacy.
16	El S	new talks collapse.
18	El S	IMF approves $50 million loan – first for eight years.
25	El S	FMLN publicly proposes state and rebel armies be replaced by single civilian police force.
26	Guate	after intense US pressure, four soldiers charged with murder of Michael Devine; URNG meets Church representatives in Quito.
28	El S	US military adviser Col. Eric Buckland testifies to Salvadorean judge that involvement of Col. Guillermo Benavides in UCA killings was known to high command.
Oct. 1	Hon	diplomatic relations established with USSR.
2	Nica	Daniel Ortega halts FSLN civil disobedience campaign after talks with Antonio Lacayo.
5	CR	twenty-four-hour general strike by 90,000 workers against austerity measures.
10	Nica	FSLN deputies vote in Assembly for *concertación* between government, labour and parties.
12	Guate	Supreme Court upholds banning of Ríos Montt candidacy.
15	Nica	ten killed as army removes 200 Contras attempting to occupy co-ops in Waslala and Matagalpa.
17	El S	FMLN stages three-hour attack on Ilopango air-base.
18	El S	US and Soviet governments issue joint declaration

			calling for UN-sponsored peace talks.
	19	El S	US Senate halves military aid by vote of 74 to 25.
	20	Nica	Central Bank President Francisco Mayorga sacked, as demanded by FSLN.
	26	Nica	Chamorro signs *concertación* agreement with FSLN-backed FNT union.
Nov.	8	Guate	Ríos Montt supporters seek injunction to halt elections.
		Pa	Noriega's defence lawyers demand all charges be dropped after Justice Department revealed to be tapping his phone.
	11	Guate	elections led by Jorge Carpio (UCN) with 25.72 per cent, ahead of Jorge Serrano (MAS) with 24.21 per cent; second round to be held on 6 Jan. 1991.
	12	Nica	ex-Contras killed by police in protest for land.
	20	El S	FMLN launches extensive attacks on anniversary of 1989 offensive; over one hundred government soldiers killed.
	22	Nica	Chamorro agrees to retire 500 officers and set up fund for ex-Contras, fifty of whom occupy border village of Macuelzo.
	27	Guate	government is refused membership of UN Social and Economic Council on grounds of human rights abuses; over 400 political killings in last month.
	30	Region	Union of Banana Exporting Countries (UPEB) re-organizes prior to establishment of single European market.
Dec.	1	Hon	Enforced resignation of military chief Gen. Arnulfo Cantarero López.
	2	El S	FMLN alleges military are preparing 'Plan Djakarta' involving execution of leading opposition figures.
		Guate	twenty villagers killed by garrison of Santiago Atitlán.
	4	Pa	Endara requests US troops to suppress mutiny by 150 police who control national HQ.
	6	Guate	Cerezo orders removal of Atitlán garrison and promises prosecutions.
	8	El S	Judge Zamora orders trial of three officers, two NCOs and three soldiers for UCA murders.
	15	Region	ninth presidential summit, Puntarenas, Costa Rica.
	23	El S	FMLN declares unilateral Christmas truce until 1 Jan. 1991.

1991

Jan.	1	Nica	arrest of four officers and eleven Salvadorean residents for selling Soviet weapons to the FMLN.
	2	El S	helicopter carrying US servicemen shot down by FMLN missile; two US soldiers summarily executed by rebels.

6	Guate	Serrano wins second electoral round with 68 per cent; abstention rate of 55 per cent.
9	El S	FMLN detains two of its fighters for murder of US soldiers.
10	Nica	supporters of Vice-Pres. Godoy removed from cabinet.
	Region	presidential summit at Tuxtla, Mexico, agrees establishment of free-trade zone by 1996 in collaboration with Mexico, Colombia and Venezuela.
11	Guate	Serrano promises social pact at his inauguration.
15	El S	Bush unfreezes $42.5 million military aid after execution of soldiers.
	Gulf	Iraq expelled from Kuwait by US-led 'coalition' offensive from Saudi Arabia.
23	El S	repatriation of 229 refugees from Panama.
24	Guate	GAM alleges total of 4,332 assassinations and 4,495 disappearances during Cerezo presidency (1986–91).
27	Pa	opposition parties win elections for five out of nine Assembly seats.

Feb. 1	Guate	Serrano refuses US military aid subject to human rights conditions.
2	El S	under observation of foreign press and diplomats at Perquín, FMLN hands over seventeen missiles illegally bought from Nicaraguan army.
16	Nica	ex-Contra leader Enrique Bermúdez assassinated in Managua.
19	El S	talks in San José; government continues to resist purge of military demanded by FMLN.
21	El S	assassination of left-wing congressional candidate Heriberto Robles and his wife.
25	El S	300 refugees attempt to return from Nicaragua without UNHCR support and against government's wishes.

Mar. 1	El S	death of Guillermo Ungo (MNR/FDR/CD) in Mexican hospital.
3	Nica	devaluation of the *córdoba de oro* and further economic adjustments provoke series of strikes.
6	Region	US cuts aid to Costa Rica, El Salvador and Guatemala; raises it to Panama, Honduras and Belize.
8	El S	start of FMLN pre-election ceasefire.
10	El S	National Assembly and municipal elections: in Assembly ARENA (44 per cent vote) loses majority, taking 37 of 84 seats; the PDC (31 per cent vote) 27 seats; CD (12 per cent vote) 8 seats; ARENA claims 135 victories in 262 municipalities, but allegations of fraud are widespread.
14	El S	Bush administration releases military aid.
20	Guate	talks in Campeche, Mexico, over return of 40,000 refugees.
	Nica	government–FNT talks end strike.

Apr.	4	El S	UN representative Alvaro de Soto opens three weeks of talks, Mexico.
	7	Guate	resignation of Finance Minister Irma Raquel Zelaya following death threats linked to anti-corruption campaign.
	8	Pa	Endara fires five PDC ministers, breaking ruling ADOC's alliance with the party.
	9	Region	US General Colin Powell, in Honduras, supports Salvadorean talks but says Gulf War offers alternative solution.
	12	El S	Antonio Cardenal, FMLN field commander and participant in Mexico talks, killed by army in Chalatenango; surprise visit by US Under-Secretary of State Bernard Aronson.
	16	Nica	Violeta Chamorro is first Nicaraguan president to visit US Congress since Somoza Snr in 1939.
	25	CR	free-trade agreement with Venezuela.
	27	El S	Mexico accords propose establishment of 'Truth Commission'; human rights procurator's office; military subordination to civilian authority; reduction in official control over Supreme Court appointments; reform of electoral law.
		Guate	three-day URNG–government negotiations agree agenda for future talks.
	30	El S	outgoing National Assembly approves draft of Mexico accord as prerequisite for reform of Constitution (which has to be approved by two successive assemblies to be valid).
May	1	El S	FMLN rejects amendments to Mexico accords; CD leader Rubén Zamora elected vice-president of National Assembly after nomination by Roberto D'Aubuissón; large May Day march.
	5	Guate	government withdraws recognition of intermediary commission negotiating return of refugees.
	6	El S	FMLN cuts power supplies across country.
	10	Hon	Cinchonero leadership formally renounces armed struggle.
	12	Guate	nine opposition politicians and union leaders flee country after receiving death threats.
	15	Hon	four peasants squatting land at Agua Caliente killed by vigilantes.
	24	El S	talks in Caracas fail to reach agreement.
	25	El S	police prohibit 300 from attending regional human rights conference in Morazán.
	28	Nica	government reveals existence of 1,000 'Recontras' grouped on Costa Rican border.
	29	Pa	strikes against austerity measures.
June	2	Guate	protest marches against conscription.

	6	Nica	Jinotega police chief killed by Recontras.
	12	El S	Cristiani visits Bush requesting more aid.
	13	Guate	Diana Ortiz files suit against ex-Defence Minister Gramajo.
	15	El S	talks collapse in Mexico after a week.
	17	El S	FMLN attacks Mariona prison, freeing 400 detainees.
		Pa	Legislative Assembly formally abolishes Defence Force.
	21	Guate	15,000 march commemorating National Day against Forced Disappearance.
	22	Guate	second round of URNG–government talks in Mexico.
	25	Nica	National Assembly receives list of Sandinista leaders who benefited personally from the *piñata* – the final FSLN law confirming revolutionary property expropriations.
	27	El S	Bush administration releases half of previously frozen $42 million military aid.
July	2	CR	general strike against austerity measures.
	10	Hon	Congress approves amnesty for political crimes.
	15	Region	presidential summit, San Salvador, approves free trade and agricultural agreements.
	18	El S	FMLN kidnaps ARENA leaders Guillermo Sol Bang and Gregorio Zelaya.
		Region	first summit of Latin American presidents, Guadalajara, Mexico; Fidel Castro is sharply criticized.
	19	Nica	FSLN holds first national congress.
	22	Hon	murder in San Pedro Sula of human rights activist Marco Tulio Hernández.
	24	Nica	FSLN congress retains nine-person directorate.
	25	El S	US Senate delays military aid vote until September.
		Nica	eighty Recontras attack Quilali.
	26	El S	UN observer mission (ONUSAL) starts human rights monitoring.
	30	El S	US grand jury indicts FMLN fighter 'Porfirio' for executing two US soldiers on 2 January.
	31	Nica	100 ex-Contras contracted for construction work in Kuwait.
Aug.	1	El S	government closes Institute for Regulation of Basic Goods (IRA), firing 1,200 employees.
		Guate	widespread protest at electricity price rise of 42 per cent with further increase of 48 per cent slated for December.
	5	Guate	murder of José Mérida, head of national CID, apparently by military.
		Hon	arrest of commander of First Battalion, Col. Angel Castillo Maradiaga, for rape and murder of seventeen-year-old Riccy Mabel Martínez.
	11	Guate	eleven people shot in head, Escuintla.
	15	Guate	arrest of seven soldiers for Escuintla killings.
	17	Guate	five plantation workers, including a USAID employee

			and a Costa Rican citizen, murdered in Alta Verapaz; San José demands investigation.
	18	El S	55,000 public employees strike against IRA closure.
		Mexico	PRI wins 290 of 300 congressional seats in poll called fraudulent by opposition.
	22	El S	private meeting in Costa Rica between Shafik Handal (FMLN) and Defence Minister Ponce to revive peace talks; rising incidence of cholera.
		Guate	GAM begins occupation of Congress; lasts nine days.
		USSR	collapse of Stalinist coup against Gorbachev.
	25	Nica	USA cancels $260 million debt.
Sept.	3	Pa	Noriega goes on trial in USA.
	11	El S	National Assembly ratifies constitutional amendments required by Mexican accord of April.
		Guate	full diplomatic relations established with Belize; 600 cases of cholera reported; Department of Forensic Medicine announces discovery of 108 clandestine cemeteries.
		Cuba	Gorbachev announces removal of remaining Soviet troops; Havana criticizes this decision.
		Nica	Chamorro vetoes UNO bill to annul legal property transfers favouring individual Sandinistas amongst others.
	14	Pa	extensive six-day strike against economic policy.
	16	El S	talks restored in New York under mediation of UN Secretary General Pérez de Cuellar; ONUSAL report criticizes both sides.
	17	Nica	withdrawal from World Court of suit against US for 1984 aggression.
	18	Guate	earthquake kills fifty-three and leaves 30,000 homeless.
	20	Guate	fourth round of peace talks in Mexico; resignation of Foreign Minister Arzú over recognition of Belize.
	25	El S	New York talks end with compressed agenda and establishment of civilian-dominated National Commission for Consolidation of Peace (COPAZ).
	28	El S	Col. Guillermo Benavides and Lt. Yusshy Mendoza convicted on Nov. 1989 murders in the UCA.
	30	Haiti	coup by army commander Gen. Raoul Cédras overthrows elected Pres. Jean-Bertrand Aristide.
Oct.	1	Guate	Serrano visits Bush to sign trade deal.
	5	Hon	US waives $434.6 million debt.
	8	Pa	eight officers arrested for coup plot.
	10	Cuba	opening of fourth congress of Communist Party.
	12	Guate	'Columbus Day' meeting at Xelaju (Quezaltenango) of continental 500 Years Indigenous and Popular Resistance Campaign; Danielle Mitterand attends.
	15	Hon	formal renunciation of armed struggle by FPRH.

	18	CR	40,000 students march against privatization of education.
	23	El S	US Congress approves military aid, withholding half subject to human rights improvements.
	28	Region	inauguration of Central American Parliament.
	31	Guate	resignation of Police Chief Mario Enrique Puiz, charged by Ombudsman de León with torture.
Nov.	3	El S	resumption of peace talks.
	7	Guate	US federal court in Boston finds ex-Defence Minister Gramajo guilty of human rights offences in civil case.
	9	Nica	offices of mayor of Managua and conservative organizations ransacked in riots following bombing of Carlos Fonseca's tomb.
	16	El S	FMLN declares unilateral truce on second anniversary of UCA murders.
	21	El S	government declares truce.
	25	El S	talks in Mexico on establishment of civilian police force; murder of former judge Francisco José Guerrero whilst carrying papers naming intellectual authors of UCA killings.
Dec.	6	Hon	troops break electricity workers' strike.
		Guate	high command altered 'to facilitate peace talks'; CUC and GAM protest against their exclusion.
	7	El S	100,000 at peace rally, San Salvador.
	10	El S	UN appoints ex-President of Colombia Belisario Betancur, ex-Foreign Minister of Venezuela Reinaldo Figueredo, and Prof. Thomas Buergenthal to Truth Commission, charged with investigating acts of political violence since 1981.
	12	Region	presidential summit, Tegucigalpa.
	19	El S	eleven Honduran soldiers killed when their helicopter shot down by FMLN over Morazán.
		Nica	Club of Paris waives $623 million of debt.

1992

Jan.	1	El S	military suspend all offensive activity.
		Guate	1991 ombudsman's report notes 6,295 denunciations received (including 228 political killings; 45 disappearances); 1,932 violations verified.
	16	Nica	government accord with Recontras and Recompas for disarming by 3 Feb.
		El S	formal and definitive peace treaty signed in Mexico City.
	21	El S	National Assembly approves general political amnesty.
		Nica	Gen. Humberto Ortega awards military decoration to

			US military attaché Col. Dennis Quinn; many Sandinistas protest.
	23	USA	Supreme Court rules that those sheltering from forced conscription in Central America are not entitled to political asylum.
	24	El S	Col. Benavides and Lt. Mendoza sentenced to thirty years for UCA murders.
	31	Guate	US State Dept. issues report critical of human rights position.
Feb.	1	El S	ceasefire comes into formal effect.
	4	Guate	police kill six on bus, Pochutá, Sololá; start of extensive counter-insurgency offensive in north and on Pacific coast.
	6	Nica	publication of platform by 'centrist' FSLN faction supporting privatization and structural adjustment.
	7	Pa	Endara alleges police coup thwarted.
	17	Nica	Miskitos belonging to YATAMA group seize Waspán, demanding removal of local authorities.
	20	El S	death of Roberto D'Aubuissón from throat cancer.
	21	Nica	disarmament programme has cost $2.5 million and yielded 10,000 weapons; an estimated 80,000 still remain in the public domain; government offers $100–200 per weapon.
Mar.	2	El S	government announces redistribution of 42,300 acres to former rebels.
	3	El S	government formally disbands Guardia Nacional and Policía de Hacienda under January accord timetable, but many former members are transferred to Policía Nacional.
	4	Hon	Congress approves neo-liberal Agricultural Modernization Law, effectively ending agrarian reform.
	6	Nica	over 1,000 Recontras and Recompas occupy Ocotal, demanding land.
	13	El S	FMLN announces that two fighters accused of murdering US advisers in Jan. 1991 will be handed over to the courts.
	18	Region	presidential summit in Antigua agrees to align tariffs within ninety days.
	20	El S	US denies visa to FMLN leader Joaquín Villalobos.
	22	Region	Inter-American Development Bank announces $1 billion in credits.
	23	Nica	Daniel Ortega cancels trip to World Bank to mediate threatened FNT strike.
		El S	World Bank 'rewards' peace process with $800 million over two years.
	28	Nica	Recontras kill five in dispute over land.
	31	Nica	government–FSLN talks on 'social crisis'.
		Guate	police evict over 1,000 Cakchiquel people squatting abandoned *finca* they claim to be ancestral land.

Apr.	1	El S	final group of 850 refugees from Mesa Grande returns; PCS and UDN formally end alliance of twenty-four years.
	4	El S	MNR withdraws from Convergencia Democrática; reported remittances by Salvadoreans in USA and Canada in 1991 amount to $435 million (in 1979: $49 million).
	7	Guate	Diana Ortiz testifies about her torture by military in 1990.
	10	Nica	eruption of Cerro Negro destroys 3,000 homes.
		Guate	police fire on student parade, killing one.
		El S	FMLN unilaterally delays demobilization on grounds of slow land distribution and bad faith over police reorganization.
	15	Guate	airforce bombs El Quiché.
	20	Nica	Recontra and Recompa troops blockade Panama highway in north.
	22	Hon	government sponsors Consejo Nacional Campesino (CNC) as peasant confederation to support new agricultural law opposed by COCOCH.
	23	El S	National Assembly breaks peace accord by reforming – rather than repealing – 1933 decree establishing Guardia Nacional and Policía de Hacienda.
	30	Guate	150 minors arrested after three days of student demos demanding more resources for schools.
May	1	Guate	70,000 commemorate labour day – largest demonstration in years.
	6	Guate	in unprecedented overturn of appeal, court sentences four police officers to jail for beating street child Nahamán Carmona to death.
	7	Hon	Frente Morazanista de Liberación Nacional formally abandons armed struggle.
	8	Guate	police clash with secondary students; 150 arrests and two deaths.
	12	El S	UDN joins Convergencia Democrática (CD).
	14	El S	US extends Temporary Protective Status (TPS) to refugees for twelve months beyond June deadline.
	15	Guate	URNG issues new peace platform.
	20	Hon	army starts eviction of occupations of fallow land in ten departments by COCOCH members demanding tenure under old agrarian reform law.
	21	Region	EC rejects requests to alter new banana tariff.
	23	El S	FMLN declares itself a political party.
	27	El S	Justice Department starts investigation of 1981 El Mozote massacre.
	30	Nica	US Congress freezes $104 million in aid after right wing, led by Sen. Jesse Helms, demands changes in control of military and return of expropriated property.

June	1	El S	ANDES teachers' union strikes.
	3	El S	UN Security Council criticizes government and FMLN for non-compliance with peace accords.
	5	Nica	UNO leadership attacks Chamorro as anti-democratic in her de facto alliance with the FSLN.
	7	Guate	government announces closure of National Housing Bank.
	10	Nica	Congress reforms penal code, increasing sentences for rape, and placing sodomy on the same legal basis.
	11	Pa	visit by Pres. Bush; demonstrations oblige him to abandon speech.
	13	Guate	death in Cobán of wealthy entrepreneur Edgar Gálvez Peña, allegedly involved in narcotics.
	19	Nica	Arnaldo Alemán, conservative mayor of Managua, announces relocation to countryside of fifty-five of 180 squatter communities in capital.
	23	Guate	public sector strike.
	29	Pa	Congress approves constitutional reforms, including abolition of the military.
	30	El S	one-fifth of FMLN troops demobilized.
		Guate	Serrano rebuffs URNG's proposals.
		Nica	forty families evicted from Matagalpa plantation by troops enforcing reversal of agrarian reform that has affected 4,000 peasants in last twelve weeks.
July	1	Guate	application of 7 per cent VAT on wide range of basic goods and services.
	3	El S	forty-eight-hour public sector national strike.
	6	El S	ANDES strike ends after thirty-four days following government agreement with *oficialista* FMS union.
	12	El S	forty-eight-hour general strike against VAT, for pay rises and participation of private sector (ANEP) in Economic and Social Forum.
	21	Guate	police break up legally authorized peasant demonstration with violence; Interior Minister Fernando Hurtado resigns; according to the Archbishop's human rights office the first six months of 1992 saw 190 disappearances.
	24	Hon	discovery in Colomancagua of mutilated body of Juan Humberto Sánchez, seized by army two weeks earlier.
Aug.	2	El S	FMLN suspends demobilization following assassination of union leader Ivan Ramírez.
	7	Guate	peace talks reach partial agreement over freezing civil patrols.
		El S	attempted assassination of Reyes Tomás Martínez, FMLN's director for reconstruction in eastern zone.
	10	El S	truth Commission opens offices.
	12	Guate	release of soldiers charged with 1991 Escuintla killings 'for lack of evidence'.

	13	El S	UN Secretary Adjunct Marrack Goulding declares indefinite extension of ONUSAL mandate.
		Hon	budget for 1993 15 per cent lower than current year, but defence spending increased (by $1.7 million); 3,000 confirmed cases of AIDS – highest in region.
	20	Guate	Human Rights Commission reports 1,111 violations, including 373 extrajudicial killings, over last eight months.
		Region	Central American and Mexican governments sign free trade accord.
	27	Guate	large demonstration in Sololá against civil patrols.
		El S	joint march by ex-combatants of FMLN and state armies demanding land and jobs.
Sept.	1	Guate	electricity prices rise 50 per cent.
		El S	FMLN becomes legal party.
		Nica	tidal wave on Pacific coast kills 160 and damages 20,000 homes.
	2	Nica	majority of deputies leave to assist in relief effort; Pres. of Assembly Alfredo César calls in replacement deputies and proceeds to table series of controversial bills.
	5	Nica	Chief of Police René Vivas and twelve commanders replaced in apparent deal with US.
	9	El S	Economic and Social Forum – established under peace accord – opens five months late.
	11	Hon	World Court settles long-standing territorial dispute with El Salvador, awarding two-thirds of contested land to Honduras.
	16	El S	Secretary General opens UN official evaluation of peace process.
	18	Pa	series of bomb explosions precedes arrest of ex-FDP members.
		Nica	army disarms 950 Recontras in north.
	21	El S	FMLN demobilizes second fifth of troops.
	23	Guate	agreement on terms for return of refugees from Mexico.
		El S	Ad Hoc Commission presents findings to UN Secretary General.
	29	Hon	Congress passes hastily drafted bill repealing legislation that prohibits army commander from holding office for more than three years; Gen. Discua Elvir's term falls due in Jan. 1993.
Oct.	7	Region	North American Free Trade Agreement (NAFTA) signed by USA, Canada and Mexico.
	9	Cuba	US government passes 'Cuba Democracy Act' extending trade embargo to US companies based in Europe; EC protests.
	10	Guate	US Congress makes 1993 aid appropriation of $30 million conditional on improvements in human rights.

	11	El S	FMLN commander Pablo Andino severely wounded in assassination attempt.
	12	Guate	GAM offices bombed.
	16	Guate	Rigoberta Menchú awarded Nobel Peace Prize.
	23	El S	UN proposal rescheduling peace agreement to 15 Dec. deadline accepted by FMLN, rejected by government.
		USA	deportation of Salvadorean death squad defector César Vielman Joya despite threats.
	29	El S	Cristiani accepts UN proposal to extend deadline from 31 Oct. to 15 Dec.
	31	El S	forensic investigation of 1981 El Mozote massacre reveals fifty-eight cadavers of children under eleven years; FMLN demobilizes third fifth of troops.
Nov.	4	USA	Bill Clinton wins election.
	7	El S	agreement on year-end deadline for purging human rights violators from armed forces.
	9	Guate	six police officers charged with killing students in April.
	14	El S	unexpected two-day visit by US Chief of Staff Gen. Powell.
	15	Pa	'No' majority in referendum on constitutional reform, including abolition of military.
	16	El S	Jesuit order requests freedom for those jailed for UCA killings.
	17	El S	remains of over one hundred children now excavated at El Mozote.
	19	El S	two UCA students murdered.
	20	El S	FMLN starts demobilization of fourth fifth of troops.
	21	Guate	airforce bombs El Quiché.
	23	Nica	assassination of Arges Sequiera, president of rightist Association of Expropriated Nicaraguans.
	24	El S	FMLN halt demobilization until Cristiani complies with UN requirement for suspension of 150 officers suspected of violating human rights.
		Cuba	UN General Assembly votes 59 to 3 for a repeal of new US embargo.
	27	Nica	Supreme Court rules null and void actions of Assembly since Sept. takeover by César.
	28	Guate	country again refused membership of UN Social and Economic Council.
	30	El S	independent Human Rights Commission publishes list of 239 army officers accused of crimes; UN Security Council extends ONUSAL mandate until May 1993.
Dec.	2	El S	FMLN begins to destroy its weapons.
		Nica	US releases half of $104 million aid frozen since June.
	8	El S	Atlacatl Battalion – responsible for El Mozote massacre and UCA killings – disbanded.
	10	El S	Assembly approves judicial and electoral reforms; FMLN gains legal authority to broadcast.

15	El S	US waives three-quarters of $615 million debt to federal agencies.
18	Guate	Nobel laureate Rigoberta Menchú 'temporarily' deposits her medal for safe-keeping in Mexico.
24	USA	outgoing Pres. Bush pardons Iran-Contra affair principals.
29	Nica	Pres. Chamorro rules César in contempt of court and convenes Assembly for 9 January.

1993

Jan.	1	El S	government fails to meet deadline for purging human rights violators from military.
	3	Guate	Human Rights Commission declares 500 extrajudicial killings and disappearances occurred in 1992.
	4	El S	FMLN suspends destruction of anti-aircraft missiles in protest at government failure to purge military.
		Hon	Gen. Discua appointed to second term; civilian control of military eroded.
	8	El S	Atonal Battalion disbanded.
	9	Nica	Chamorro appoints former Communist and UNO centrist Gustavo Tablada as new president of National Assembly; UNO split is formalised with twelve of fourteen parties now in opposition to government.
	10	Guate	URNG presents new peace plan.
	11	El S	UN reports that Cristiani has accepted need for dismissal of eighty-seven officers named by Ad Hoc Commission; fifteen cases pending.
	20	Guate	Serrano presents new peace plan; first group of 2,500 returning refugees, accompanied by UNCHR, met by Rigoberta Menchú at border.
	21	Guate	URNG rejects Serrano's ninety-day limit on peace talks.
	25	Hon	SITRATERCO ends three-week strike affecting 7,000 United Brands workers after company agrees to maintain plantation.
	28	Guate	report by Ombudsman de León Carpio notes allegations of 387 extrajudicial killings and 99 disappearances (compared with 553 and 112 respectively in 1991).
Feb.	1	Region	establishment of Central American Integration System (SICA).
	6	Hon	US State Dept. report criticizes human rights abuses by military; 2,000 troops deployed in San Pedro Sula.
	11	Region	eight Latin American banana-producing countries condemn EC import quotas.
	12	Guate	Noel de Jesús Beteta, formerly of presidential military staff, sentenced to twenty-five years for murder of Myrna Mack in Sept. 1990.
	20	Region	first Central American drug summit, Belize.

	24	Cuba	first direct, secret-ballot, single-candidate elections to National Assembly; Castro hints at retirement.
Mar.	1	Hon	Callejas establishes Ad Hoc Commission for reform of judiciary and DNI police.
	8	Nica	ultra-rightist 'Yolaina' commando seizes embassy in San José for thirteen days, demanding new command for EPS and money for Recontras.
	12	Nica	presidential minister Antonio Lacayo urges UNO to talk.
		El S	Defence Minister Gen. Ponce presents resignation.
	15	El S	publication of 600-page Truth Commission report on political crimes since 1981; leading military figures named.
	20	El S	Assembly approves by 47 votes to 9 (13 abstentions; 15 absent) a general political amnesty for all those involved in political crimes committed during the civil war, including those named in Truth Commission report.
	21	Nica	last hostages leave San José embassy; Ambassador Alfonso Robelo attacks government of his old ally Chamorro.
		El S	US Secretary of State Warren Christopher appoints commission to investigate US involvement in civil war under Reagan administration.
		Guate	presidential press spokesman Fernando Muñiz threatens media with censorship.
	23	Region	Guatemala, El Salvador and Honduras sign 'Northern Triangle' integration agreement, allowing free transit of goods and persons from 1 April.
		El S	Defence Minister Ponce describes Truth Commission report 'unethical and disrespectful' and an insult to the armed forces.
	24	Guate	divided Congress agrees to present attorney general with evidence of extensive public sector corruption, including important Serrano associates.
		Pa	Supreme Court rules unconstitutional article 373 of labour code which requires payroll deductions of union dues; extensive labour mobilization over wages.
		CR	conflict within PLN over candidacy of José María Figueres for 1994 poll.
	26	El S	Supreme Court attacks Truth Commission report for 'damaging the dignity of the justice system'.
		Hon	Callejas, pre-empting Ad Hoc Commission, announces transfer of DNI to civilian control.
	27–8	Nica	closed FSLN assembly reflects sharp criticism of party leadership.
	30	Nica	Assembly approves, after four months' delay, budget for 1993 at $423 million – a reduction in real expenditure.
		Guate	mediator Bishop Quezada Toruño declares government–URNG talks at an impasse.

Apr. 1 El S Col. Benavides and Lt. Mendoza released under amnesty.

2 Guate Judge Eulalio González Amaya gravely wounded in assassination attempt, prompting controversial Supreme Court decision to transfer entire Court of Jalapa to capital.

3 Nica US releases $50 million aid frozen for ten months; Club of Paris agrees $630 million package.

8 CR Assembly votes 32 to 15 for Rodrigo Carazo Zeledón to become first holder of post of People's Defender (ombudsman).

11 Guate two-day riot at Pavoncito prison; seven killed; Noel de Jesús Beteta escapes.

Pa Endara administration opposes broad amnesty proposed in Assembly by PRD for supporters of ousted Noriega regime (sixty jailed and forty in exile).

12 Hon Ad Hoc Commission report recommendations include establishment by Jan. 1994 of an independent public ministry to oversee constitutional guarantees; replacement of DNI by civilian DIC; extensive reform of FUSEP.

13 El S sixth report on human rights by ONUSAL indicates improvements over period June 1992 to Jan. 1993 despite 106 killings and 165 death threats amongst the 1,480 denunciations made to the mission.

15 Hon legislative commission set up to investigate child-trafficking following campaign by deputy Rosario Godoy de Osejo and revelation of several harrowing cases.

El S campaign to prolong for eighteen months the Temporary Protective Status (TPS) introduced by US in Sept. 1990 for illegal immigrants and due to end on 30 June.

CR Assembly approves three laws to depoliticize judicial appointments and professionalize legal system.

Nica UNO agrees to participate in 'National Dialogue'; its team to be led by Managua mayor Arnaldo Alemán.

19 Guate episcopal conference in Quezaltenango sharply criticizes government and offers support to Communities of Populations in Resistance.

20 Nica FSLN presents eighteen-point economic programme to government.

23 Nica government joins 'Northern Triangle' agreement, liberalizing movement of people from 1 May and of goods from 1 June.

24 CR five men hold for five days twenty-six Supreme Court judges and employees, purporting to be Colombian *narcotraficantes* and demanding $20 million in ransom; captured at airport and revealed to be ex-policemen.

26 Guate controversial government-organized 'Summit of Latin

American Intellectuals' in Antigua shunned by leading figures.

28 El S ARENA convention elects Armando Calderón Sol as 1994 presidential candidate.

30 Guate ten people massacred, San Pedro Jacopilas, Quiché; Ombudsman de León Carpio orders investigation.

May 1 Guate URNG closes five days of attacks in San Marcos, Retalhuleu, and Quiché; 50,000-strong May Day march includes policemen demanding union rights, demonstrates against electricity, transport price rises and forced recruitment.

3 Nica government opens four days of talks with main parties and civic bodies as part of 'National Dialogue'.

El S Shafik Handal declares that FMLN will not present candidate for 1994 presidential election.

5 Guate Appeal Court dismisses charges against six soldiers for Escuintla killings of August 1991 on grounds of lack of evidence.

8 Guate government–URNG talks in Mexico collapse after twenty minutes; mediator Bishop Quezada criticizes intransigence on both sides over conditions for ceasefire.

9 Guate elections in 276 of 330 municipalities (84 per cent of national electorate) produce good results for ruling MAS but with very low turn-out; government proposals for withdrawal of subsidies of transport, fuel and electricity prices draw open opposition from DCG and UCN in Congress.

11 Guate teenager killed by congressional bodyguards during disturbances in capital centre caused by protests against enforcement of school uniforms and ID cards for free public transport.

13 Guate bus services in capital shut down, with thirty-five destroyed over last fortnight; Capt. Hugo Roberto Contreras, jailed for murder of Michael Devine, escapes from Mariscal Zavala Brigade two days after being sentenced to twenty-five years.

Hon Attorney General Leonardo Matute Murillo unconstitutionally removed from office by PN deputies – PL abstains – on grounds of conflict of interest.

18 Nica Chamorro suspends constitutional guarantees for thirty days in north and centre of country, where more than a dozen armed bands are operating.

Guate riot police battle with 800 students outside USAC campus; influential Chiquimula deputy Obdulio Chinchilla wounded in assassination attempt.

20 El S national police kill at least one person in repression of demonstration by disabled veterans of army (ALFAES) and FMLN (ASALDIG) demanding release of land and

137

			benefits due six months earlier.
	21	Guate	Serrano announces establishment of new anti-riot squad; 10,000-strong rally in capital demands his resignation.
	23	El S	large explosion destroys FMLN arms cache in Managua.
	25	Guate	Serrano suspends forty-six articles of the Constitution, dissolves Congress, Supreme Court and Court of Constitutionality, charging their control by corrupt interests and the mafia; announces elections for a new constituent assembly in sixty days.
	26	Guate	Court of Constitutionality formally annuls and declares criminal Serrano's *autogolpe*; President of Supreme Court Juan José Rodil Peralta and President of Congress José Lobo Dubón placed under home arrest; Ombudsman Ramiro de León Carpio goes underground; US, EC and Japan halt aid.
	27	Guate	troops break up protest against coup by court employees; censorship imposed; open opposition voiced by Church, CACIF and Amigos del País as well as popular organizations.
	28	Guate	*Crónica* distributed by hand, police take no action; Ombudsman de León Carpio breaks cover formally to close his office in front of international press.
	13	Guate	Serrano meets high command after talks with OAS Secretary General João Baena Soares over sanctions tabled for ratification in three days; appears on TV accompanied by Defence Minister Gen. José Domingo García Samayoa to deny resignation rumours.
June	1	Guate	Gen. García declares that Serrano has resigned along with Vice-President Gustavo Espina Salguero; Court of Constitutionality will choose a successor; demonstrations against coup unmolested by police.
	2	Guate	Serrano flees to El Salvador; Espina denies any resignation, declares himself president, and is endorsed by Gen. García; Espina calls on Congress to ratify his position but after five hours (at 11 p.m.) only forty-four of the quorum requirement of seventy-nine appear; US emphatically denies claims Espina has its support.
	3	Guate	military spokesman Capt. Julio Alberto Yon refuses to endorse Espina as demos and CACIF demand his removal; police do not intervene.
	4	Guate	Espina continues to seek congressional support, splitting DCG; general strike; Archbishop Penados de Barrio reiterates article 186 of Constitution, which prohibits coup authors from holding executive office; Rigoberta Menchú proposes Church mediation; army describes her as 'irresponsible'.
	5	Guate	Court of Constitutionality declares Espina incompetent

and calls on Congress to choose the new president; Gen. García promises military will not interfere.

6   Guate   in second round of congressional voting Ramiro de León Carpio is elected president, after withdrawal of 81-year-old president of electoral tribunal Arturo Herbruger.

7   Guate   de León fires Gen. García and alters high command; US restores aid.

Appendix 2 Costa Rica: Profile

	1982	1983	1984	1985	1986	1987	1988	1989	1990	1991	1992ᵖ
Population (thousands)	2,421	2,493	2,566	2,642	2,716	2,791	2,866	2,941	3,015	3,088	3,165
Gross Domestic Product (millions of 1988 dollars)	3,674	3,772	4,066	4,098	4,319	4,515	4,658	4,905	5,081	5,138	5,344
GDP Per Head (1988 dollars)	1,517	1,513	1,584	1,551	1,590	1,618	1,625	1,668	1,685	1,664	1,689
Exports (goods, f.o.b millions of dollars)	869.0	852.5	997.5	939.1	1,084.8	1,106.7	1,180.7	1,333.4	1,365.6	1,487.3	1,765.4
Exports Per Capita ($ US)	359	342	389	355	399	396	412	453	453	482	558
Imports (goods, f.o.b millions of dollars)	804.9	894.3	992.9	1,001.0	1,045.2	1,245.2	1,278.6	1,572.0	1,833.3	1,680.3	2,182.7
Disbursed External Debt (millions of dollars)	3,641.0	4,177.2	3,987.9	4,398.7	4,574.7	4,720.1	4,543.8	4,603.2	3,772.0	3,966.2	4,075.0
Exchange Rate (domestic currency unit per US dollar)	37.4	41.1	44.5	50.5	56.0	62.8	75.8	81.5	91.6	122.4	136.2ᵃ
Inflation Rate (average annual growth rate of consumer prices)	89.9	10.7	17.3	10.9	15.4	16.4	25.3	10.0	27.3	25.3	18.1
Real Effective Exchange Rate (1985=100)	115	96	98	100	107	112	117	110	112	121	116

Notes: p. preliminary.
    a. figure refers to end of December; taken from *Latin American Weekly Report*, 7.1.93.
Sources: *Economic and Social Progress in Latin America 1992 Report* (Inter-American Development Bank), pp. 73, 285, 286; and *Preliminary Overview of the Economy of Latin America and the Caribbean 1992* (United Nations, Economic Commission for Latin America and the Caribbean).

Appendix 3 El Salvador: Profile

	1982	1983	1984	1985	1986	1987	1988	1989	1990	1991	1992ᵖ
Population (thousands)	4,625	4,663	4,707	4,768	4,846	4,934	5,032	5,138	5,252	5,376	5,839
Gross Domestic Product (millions of 1988 dollars)	4,771	4,823	4,917	4,998	5,032	5,153	5,231	5,315	5,477	5,688	5,944
GDP Per Head (1988 dollars)	1,032	1,034	1,045	1,048	1,038	1,044	1,040	1,034	1,043	1,058	1,083
Exports (goods, f.o.b millions of dollars)	699.6	758.0	725.9	679.0	777.9	589.6	610.6	557.5	581.5	588.0	585.0
Exports Per Capita ($ US)	151	163	154	142	161	119	121	109	111	109	107
Imports (goods, f.o.b millions of dollars)	799.8	832.2	914.5	895.0	902.3	938.7	966.5	1,220.2	1,137.3	1,266.7	1,404.8
Disbursed External Debt (millions of dollars)	1,442.5	1,739.9	1,826.0	1,854.4	1,850.5	1,975.4	1,986.9	2,070.3	2,132.6	2,172.3	2,315.0
Exchange Rate (domestic currency unit per US dollar)	2.5	2.5	2.5	2.5	5.0	5.0	5.0	5.0	8.0	8.1	8.5ᵃ
Inflation Rate (average annual growth rate of consumer prices)	11.7	15.5	9.1	31.9	30.3	19.6	18.2	23.5	19.3	9.8	16.8
Real Effective Exchange Rate (1985=100)	132	135	117	100	162	139	122	105	119	134	135

Notes: p. preliminary.
   a. figure refers to end of December; taken from *Latin American Weekly Report*, 7.1.93.
Sources: *Economic and Social Progress in Latin America 1992 Report* (Inter-American Development Bank), pp. 95, 285, 286; and *Preliminary Overview of the Economy of Latin America and the Caribbean 1992* (United Nations, Economic Commission for Latin America and the Caribbean).

Appendix 4   Guatemala: Profile

	1982	1983	1984	1985	1986	1987	1988	1989	1990	1991	1992P
Population (thousands)	7,315	7,542	7,740	7,963	8,195	8,434	8,681	8,935	9,197	9,467	9,732
Gross Domestic Product (millions of 1988 dollars)	7,376	7,188	7,222	7,179	7,189	7,444	7,734	8,039	8,290	8,559	8,901
GDP Per Head (1988 dollars)	1,008	955	933	902	877	883	891	900	901	904	915
Exports (goods, f.o.b millions of dollars)	1,170.4	1,091.7	1,132.2	1,059.7	1,043.8	977.9	1,073.3	1,126.1	1,211.5	1,234.8	1,315.1
Exports Per Capita ($ US)	160	148	146	133	127	116	124	126	132	130	135
Imports (goods, f.o.b millions of dollars)	1,284.3	1,056.0	1,182.2	1,076.7	875.7	1,333.2	1,413.2	1,048.4	1,428.0	1,663.5	2,082.8
Disbursed External Debt (millions of dollars)	1,537.3	1,799.3	2,353.2	2,653.5	2,768.2	2,768.9	2,605.0	2,594.0	2,776.7	2,781.7	2,565.0
Exchange Rate (domestic currency unit per US dollar)	1.0	1.0	1.0	1.0	1.9	2.5	2.6	2.8	4.5	5.0	5.3[a]
Inflation Rate (average annual growth rate of consumer prices)	0.3	15.4	7.2	27.9	21.4	9.3	12.3	20.2	59.6	10.2	11.6
Real Effective Exchange Rate (1985=100)	120	118	113	100	142	185	186	188	220	192	193

Notes: P. preliminary.
   a. figure refers to end of December; taken from *Latin American Weekly Report*, 7.1.93.
Sources: *Economic and Social Progress in Latin America 1992 Report* (Inter-American Development Bank), pp. 101, 285, 286; and *Preliminary Overview of the Economy of Latin America and the Caribbean 1992* (United Nations, Economic Commission for Latin America and the Caribbean).

Appendix 5 Honduras: Profile

	1982	1983	1984	1985	1986	1987	1988	1989	1990	1991	1992ᵖ
Population (thousands)	3,939	4,085	4,234	4,383	4,531	4,679	4,829	4,982	5,138	5,298	5,473
Gross Domestic Product (millions of 1988 dollars)	3,103	3,082	3,206	3,352	3,387	3,593	3,769	3,913	3,915	3,995	4,175
GDP Per Head (1988 dollars)	788	754	757	765	748	768	780	785	762	754	763
Exports (goods, f.o.b millions of dollars)	676.5	698.7	737.0	789.6	891.2	844.3	893.0	966.7	847.8	832.8	911.9
Exports Per Capita ($ US)	172	171	174	180	197	180	185	194	165	157	165
Imports (goods, f.o.b millions of dollars)	680.7	756.3	884.8	879.2	874.0	893.8	916.6	964.0	869.7	853.2	839.0
Disbursed External Debt (millions of dollars)	1,841.9	2,125.0	2,283.5	2,728.1	2,973.1	3,302.3	3,304.5	3,332.9	3,480.1	3,613.5	3,160.0ᵃ
Exchange Rate (domestic currency unit per US dollar)	2.0	2.0	2.0	2.0	2.0	2.0	2.0	2.0	4.0	5.4	5.4ᵇ
Inflation Rate (average annual growth rate of consumer prices)	9.5	7.2	2.7	4.2	3.2	2.9	6.6	2.0	36.4	21.4	5.4
Real Effective Exchange Rate (1985=100)	117	108	101	100	109	117	118	109	195	200	157

Notes: p. preliminary.
   a. Excludes the official debt write-off by the United States, Switzerland and Holland of $448.4 million.
   b. figure refers to end of December; taken from *Latin American Weekly Report*, 7.1.93.

Sources: *Economic and Social Progress in Latin America 1992 Report* (Inter-American Development Bank), pp. 121, 285, 286; and *Preliminary Overview of the Economy of Latin America and the Caribbean 1992* (United Nations, Economic Commission for Latin America and the Caribbean).

143

Appendix 6 Nicaragua: Profile

	1982	1983	1984	1985	1986	1987	1988	1989	1990	1991	1992ᵖ
Population (thousands)	2,957	3,058	3,163	3,272	3,384	3,501	3,622	3,745	3,871	4,000	4,156
Gross Domestic Product (millions of 1988 dollars)	2,517	2,611	2,534	2,414	2,368	2,344	2,010	1,937	1,961	1,939	1,949
GDP Per Head (1988 dollars)	851	854	801	738	700	670	555	517	506	485	469
Exports (goods, f.o.b millions of dollars)	406.0	451.9	412.4	305.1	257.8	295.1	235.7	310.7	331.5	266.2	233.5
Exports Per Capita ($ US)	137	148	130	93	76	84	65	83	86	67	56
Imports (goods, f.o.b millions of dollars)	723.5	742.3	735.3	794.1	677.4	734.4	718.3	547.3	569.7	680.6	722.1
Disbursed External Debt (millions of dollars)	2,912.9	4,058.5	4,751.4	5,735.9	6,730.0	7,863.8	8,857.2	9,568.3	10,496.9	10,675.8	11,200.0
Exchange Rate (domestic currency unit per US dollar)ᵃ	10.1	10.1	10.1	28.0	70.0	70.0	920.0	38,150.0	3,000.0	25,000.0	5.0ᵇ
Inflation Rate (average annual growth rate of consumer prices)	24.8	35.5	47.3	334.3	747.4	1,347.2	33,547.6	1,689.1	13,490.2	775.4	2.2
Real Effective Exchange Rate (1985=100)	217	164	117	100	38	10	184	220	169	162	162

Notes: p. preliminary.
a. córdobas per thousand dollars through 1987, per dollar in 1988–89, and thousand córdobas per dollar in 1990–91; the 1992 figure refers to new currency unit (córdoba oro); end of period rate.
b. figure refers to end of December; taken from *Latin American Weekly Report*, 7.1.93.

Sources: Economic and Social Progress in Latin America 1992 Report (Inter-American Development Bank), pp. 139, 285, 286; and *Preliminary Overview of the Economy of Latin America and the Caribbean 1992* (United Nations, Economic Commission for Latin America and the Caribbean).

Appendix 7 US Economic Aid to Central America, 1980–93 (Fiscal Years; $ mn)[a]

	CR	El S	Guate	Hon	Nica	C. Am.
1980	14.0	57.8	11.1	51.0	37.1	171.0
1981	13.3	113.6	16.6	33.9	59.7	237.1
1982	51.7	182.2	15.5	80.7	6.3	336.4
1983	214.1	245.6	29.7	106.0	—	595.4
1984	169.9	215.9	20.3	95.0	0.1	501.2
1985	220.0	433.9	106.9	229.0	—	989.7
1986	148.0	315.4	105.5	124.0	—	692.9
1987	116.8	508.9	116.4	128.7	—	870.8
1988	105.4	314.1	137.3	156.8	—	713.6
1989	113.6	307.0	146.2	80.2	—	647.0
1990	83.0	245.2	117.5	188.2	300.0	933.9
1991	48.2	215.0	85.1	101.7	193.2	643.2
1992[b]	38.0	207.8	82.1	108.4	204.0	640.3
1993[b]	28.0	245.0	55.8	81.6	189.2	599.7

Notes: a. Includes development aid; PL480 (subsidized food sales and grants); Peace Corps; narcotics control; disaster relief; Economic Support Funds (ESF).
   b. Executive request to Congress.

Sources: Caution should be taken with the precision of these figures, which have been rounded to the nearest decimal point. Figures 1980–87 are disbursed, but even these vary somewhat between secondary sources since contemporary reports issued by the State Department (and usually relayed through the Congressional Research Service, Library of Congress) are often subject to amendment, not least by executive or congressional decision to freeze or withdraw funds.

   Sources employed here are as follows: for all countries 1980–87: R. Fagen et al., *Forging Peace. The Challenge of Central America*, New Haven 1987, pp. 149–51; Costa Rica, 1988–90: *Central American Report* (CAR), 30.7.91; Guatemala, 1988–90: CAR, 26.7.91; Honduras, 1988–90: CAR, 14.6.91; El Salvador, 1988–90: Americas Watch, *El Salvador's Decade of Terror*, New Haven 1991, p. 141; all countries, 1991: WOLA briefing, 4.2.91; all countries, 1992: CAR, 8.3.91; all countries, 1993: CAR, 6.5.92.

Appendix 8 US Military Aid to Central America, 1980–93 (Fiscal Years; $ mn)[a]

	CR	El S	Guate	Hon	Nica	C. Am.
1980	—	5.9	—	3.9	—	9.8
1981	—	35.5	—	8.9	—	44.4
1982	2.1	82.0	—	31.3	—	115.6
1983	4.6	81.1	—	47.3	—	133.0
1984	9.1	196.6	—	77.4	—	283.1
1985	11.2	136.3	0.5	67.4	—	215.4
1986	2.6	121.7	5.4	61.1	—	190.8
1987	1.7	116.0	5.4	61.2	—	184.3
1988	0.2	81.5	9.4	41.2	—	132.3
1989	0.2	81.4	9.4	41.1	—	132.1
1990	1.8	81.0	3.3	21.3	—	107.4
1991	0.2	85.0	2.4	23.1	—	110.7
1992[b]	2.6	86.4	2.4	20.2	—	111.6
1993[b]	1.2	41.4	0.4	9.7	—	52.7

Notes: a. Includes International Military Education and Training (IMET); Foreign Military Sales (credit); Military Assistance Program (MAP).
   b. Executive request to Congress.

Sources: As for Appendix 7. It should be noted that Fagen et al., *Forging Peace*, assign Economic Support Funds (ESF) to military aid whereas here ESF funds are treated (as in almost all texts) as economic aid.

Appendix 9   The Military in Central America

	1977/80[1]	1985[2]	1991[3]
Costa Rica			
troops[4]	5,000	9,800	8,000
vehicles[5]	—	—	—
aircraft[6]	—	—	—
mil. budget ($ mn)			39.0
mil. budget (% total)	2.7	5.4	2.7
social budget (% total)[7]	56.3	26.0	31.9
El Salvador			
troops	7,130	51,150	56,000
vehicles	32	73	
aircraft	68	155	
mil. budget ($ mn)			145.5
mil. budget (% total)	8.7	27.3	17.8
social budget (% total)	30.3	24.5	23.2
Guatemala			
troops	14,300	51,600	60,000
vehicles	41	71	
aircraft	35	83	
mil. budget ($ mn)			91.0
mil. budget (% total)	8.6	19.4	8.0
social budget (% total)	14.0	20.9	20.0
Honduras			
troops	14,200	21,700	27,000
vehicles		59	
aircraft	44	90	
mil. budget ($ mn)			40.0
mil. budget (% total)	8.7	6.5	7.3
social budget (% total)	25.4	27.5	28.7
Nicaragua			
troops	7,100	61,800	28,000
vehicles	50	195	
aircraft	8	75	
mil. budget ($ mn)			70.0
mil. budget (% total)	13.0	38.0	8.6
social budget (% total)	40.9	20.1	37.9

Notes: 1. Troop strengths are for 1977; all other entries for 1980. *Source*: Ricardo Córdova, 'Los Efectos Económicos de la Militarización en la Región Centroamericana (1979–86)', Occasional Paper no. 20, March 1987, Latin American and Caribbean Center, Florida International University.
2. *Source*: as for note 1.
3. *Source*: troop strengths and gross budget for all countries: *Central American Report* (CAR), 15 Nov. 1991; budget percentages: El Salvador – CAR, 9 Nov. 1991; Costa Rica – CAR, 21 Sept. 1990; Honduras – CAR, 11 Oct. 1991; Guatemala – CAR, 20 Dec. 1991; Nicaragua – CAR, 23 April 1993. The budget for the Ejército Popular Sandinista was cut from $104 million in 1990 to $71 million in 1991, $42.9 million in 1992 and $36.5 million scheduled for 1993. CAR, 16 April 1993.
4. Includes all forces in regular army, airforce, navy, coast and frontier guards and paramilitary police employed by the state. Except for Costa Rica – where figures relate to all police and security functionaries – civilian police are not included in these figures. In 1991 total police forces were as follows: Costa Rica – 8,000; El Salvador – 15,000; Guatemala – 17,500; Honduras – 14,000; Nicaragua – 11,000. CAR, 15 Nov. 1991. Civilian militias and patrols organized by the state are excluded from the above figures; these organizations were of consequence in Nicaragua (approximately 60,000 in 1985) and Guatemala (c. 100,000 in 1985).
5. Includes all tanks, armoured and transport vehicles but excludes artillery pieces. *Source*: Córdova.
6. Includes all military aircraft, helicopters, trainers and reconnaissance aircraft. *Source*: Córdova.
7. Expenditures on education, health and (in the case of Costa Rica) social security.

Appendix 10 Elections in Central America, 1980–93[a]

	CR	El S	Guate	Hon	Nica	Pa
1980						
1981				Const (iv) Pres (xi)		
1982	Pres & Leg (ii)	Const (iii)				
1983						
1984		Pres (iv & v)	Const (vii)		Pres & Const (xi)	Pres & Leg (v)
1985		Leg (iii)	Pres (xi & xii)	Pres & Leg (xi)		
1986	Pres & Leg (ii)					
1987						
1988		Leg & Mpl (iii)	Mpl (iv)			
1989		Pres (iii)		Pres & Leg (xi)		Pres & Leg (v)
1990	Pres & Leg (ii)		Pres & Leg (xi)		Pres & Leg (ii)	
1991		Leg & Mpl (iii)	Pres (i)			Leg (i)
1992						
1993			Mpl (v)	Pres & Leg (xi)		

Note: a. Const is used to denote constituent assembly, regardless of whether that body continues with legislative functions subsequent to ratifying a constitution. Municipal elections are shown only for El Salvador and Guatemala, where their introduction in the 1980s was a matter of political significance. In both Guatemala and El Salvador presidential elections may be held in two rounds (as in 1990–91 and 1984 respectively) if no candidate wins an absolute majority of the vote in the first round. The legislative elections of January 1991 in Panama were partial. Roman numerals signify the month(s) in which the elections were held.

Appendix 11   Central American Elections – Synoptic Results, 1987–93
(main contestants only; percentage of votes rounded to nearest decimal point)

Costa Rica

General, February 1990 (Abstention Rate[1]: 21%)

Presidential Candidate/Party	Votes	% Vote	Cong. Seats
Rafael Angel Calderón (PUSC)	687,967	51.4	29
Carlos Castillo (PLN)	623,239	47.3	25

Source: CAR, 23 Feb. 1990.

El Salvador

i) Legislative and Municipal, March 1988 (Abstention Rate[1]: 55%)

Party	Votes	% Vote	Cong. Seats
ARENA	447,696	48.1	30
PDC	326,716	35.1	23
PCN	78,756	8.5	7

ii) Presidential, March 1989 (Abstention Rate[1]: 57%)

Candidate/Party	Votes	% Vote
Alfredo Cristiani (ARENA)	505,370	53.8
Fidel Chávez Mena (PDC)	338,369	36.0
Rafael Morán Castañeda (PCN)	38,218	4.0
Guillermo Ungo (CD)	35,642	3.8

Source: CAR, 31 March 1989.

iii) Legislative and Municipal, March 1991 (Abstention Rate[1]: 52%)

Party	Votes	% Vote	Cong. Seats
ARENA	466,091	44.3	39
PDC	294,029	27.7	26
PCN	94,531	9.0	9
CD	127,855	12.2	8
MAC	33,971	3.2	1
UDN	28,206	2.7	1

Source: CAR, 5 April 1991

Appendix 11   (cont.)

Guatemala

i) General, November 1990 (Abstention Rate[1]: 37%).

Presidential Candidate/Party	Votes	% Vote	Cong. Seats
Jorge Carpio (UCN)	399,777	25.7	41
Jorge Serrano (MAS)	375,165	24.1	18
Alfonso Cabrera (DCG)	271,933	17.5	27
Alvaro Arzú (PAN)	268,796	17.3	12
Ernesto Sosa (MLN)	74,825	4.8	4
René de León Schlotter (PSD)	55,819	3.6	1

Source: CAR, 16 and 23 Nov. 1990

ii) Presidential, second round, January 1991 (Abstention Rate[1]: 55%)

Candidate/Party	Votes	% Vote
Jorge Serrano (MAS)	936,389	68.1
Jorge Carpio (UCN)	438,990	31.9

Source: CAR, 11 Jan. 1991.

iii) Municipal, April 1988, November 1990, May 1993 (Abstention Rates[1]: 58%; 37%; 70%)

Party	Mayoralties		
	1988	1990	1993
DCG	140	86	40
UCN	55	132	37
MAS	2	13	100
PAN	—	16	33
MLN	12	10	1
PSD	1	9	4
Civic Committees	12		20

Source: CAR, 23 Nov. 1990; 14 May 1993.

Honduras

General, November 1989 (Abstention Rate[1]: 24%).

Presidential Candidate/Party	Votes	% Vote	Cong. Seats
Rafael Callejas (PN)	917,168	51	55
Carlos Flores Facusse (PL)	776,983	43	71
Enrique Aguilar Cerrato (PINU)	33,952	2	2
Efraín Diez Arrivillaga (PDC)	25,453	1	2

Source: CAR, 12 Jan. 1990.

Appendix 11   (cont.)

Nicaragua

General, February 1990 (Abstention Rate[1]: 15%).

Presidential Candidate/Party	Votes	% Vote	Cong. Seats
Violeta Chamorro (UNO)	777,552	54.7	51
Daniel Ortega (FSLN)	579,886	40.8	39
Erick Ramírez (PSC)	11,136	0.7	1
Moisés Hassán (MUR)	16,751	1.1	1

Source: *Barricada Internacional*, 10 March 1990.

Panama

General, May 1989 (annulled immediately by Gen. Noriega) and January 1991 (partial) (Abstention Rates[1]: 1989: uncertain due to widespread fraud; 1991: 49%)[2].

Party		Cong. Seats	
		May 1989	Jan. 1991
ADOC			
	PDC	26	28
	MOLIRENA	14	16
	PA	7	7
	PLA	4	4
COLINA			
	PRD	7	10
	PALA	—	1
	PL	—	1
Total		58	67

Source: CAR, 8 Feb. 1991

Notes: 1. Percentage of registered voters who cast no vote at all. This figure significantly under-represents the 'real' abstention rate because of low levels of registration, except in Costa Rica (where voting is compulsory but abstention punished lightly, if at all, with a modest fine) and, to a lesser extent, Nicaragua.
2. The 1991 poll in Panama was held for nine congressional seats and 160 municipalities, the number of congressional seats occupied rising from 58 to 67.

BOOKS FROM THE LATIN AMERICA BUREAU

PERU:TIME OF FEAR
Deborah Poole & Gerardo Rénique

Since 1980 Peru has been the scene of an escalating civil war between the Sendero Luminoso ('Shining Path') Maoists and the Peruvian military. Caught in the middle, and dying in their thousands each year, are the poor peasants and slum-dwellers of Peru. Victims also of a collapsing economy and radical austerity programme, the great majority of Peruvians are living a time of fear.

"This book offers informative, sometimes gripping narratives of Peru's political agony and violence." Steve J Stern, Director of Latin American Studies, University of Wisconsin

"I know of no more informative and realistic account in English of Sendero Luminoso, its chilling ideology, modus operandi, and prospects." Eric Hobsbawn

November 1992 212 pages, index ISBN 0 906156 70 X £9.00/US$17.00

THE LATIN AMERICAN CITY
Alan Gilbert

Looks at the region's urban explosion from the perspective of the poor. It asks why people are attracted to the city, explores options open to new arrivals and strategies for acquiring land and building a home. Highlighting the role of the informal sector in urban survival, it also explains how popular organisation and protest can result in improved living standards for the poor.

"Alan Gilbert has long been one of the most incisive and perceptive analysts of urban problems and policy in Latin America. **The Latin American City** ... is the most comprehensive of any text to date." Professor Wayne Cornelius, University of California.

January 1994 192 pages, index ISBN 0 906156 82 3 £10.00/US$17.00

COMPANERAS
Voices from the Latin American Women's movement
Gabi Kuppers (ed)

Covering thirteen Latin American countries from Brazil to Haiti, women speak for themselves about feminism and women's activism. Interviews and essays give a voice to women in indigenous organisations, refuges and advice centres, peasants movements, trade unions, political parties, as well as feminist research institutes, alternative media and a prostitutes' collective.

May 1994 200 pages, index ISBN 0 906156 86 6 £10.00/US$17.00

Prices are for paperback editions and include postage and packing

LAB books are available by post from Latin America Bureau, Dept V, 1 Amwell Street, London EC1R 1UL. Write for a free catalogue.

US$ orders for LAB books should be sent to Monthly Review Press, 122 West 27th Street, New York, NY 10001. Cheques payable to Monthly Review Press.

The Latin America Bureau is an independent research and publishing organisation. It works to broaden public understanding of human rights and social and economic justice in Latin America and the Caribbean.